HEBREWS

A Devotional Commentary

W. H. GRIFFITH THOMAS

WM. B. EERDMANS PUBLISHING COMPANY
GRAND RAPIDS, MICHIGAN

WM. B. EERDMANS PUBLISHING CO.

ISBN 0-8028-1552-9

Eighth Printing, September 1979

PHOTOLITHOPRINTED BY EERDMANS PRINTING COMPANY
GRAND RAPIDS, MICHIGAN, UNITED STATES OF AMERICA

INTRODUCTION

THIS BOOK contains the amplification of Lectures and Bible Readings which I have had the privilege of giving, first at Wycliffe Hall, Oxford, 1905-10, then at the Moody Bible Institute, Chicago, 1911, and subsequently at other Bible Institutes and at several Bible Conferences in America.

I have no intention or desire to add to the many valuable commentaries available on this Epistle, but I have thought it might be profitable to concentrate on one of the main themes (if not *the* main theme) of Hebrews, the necessity and conditions of spiritual progress. As I try to show, even though its primary message was to the Christian Jews to whom it was originally addressed, its teaching, exhortations, and warnings are directly applicable to believers today for the purpose of inciting them to possess and enjoy the fullest and highest Christian life.

With the view of obtaining all possible light on the development of this special topic, I have collected and utilized everything I could find on Hebrews, and the Bibliography will show the character and extent of my indebtedness.

A brief outline of the book was given as Bible Readings at the Keswick Convention, 1922, and since then the chapters have appeared, substantially as they are now, in the pages of *The Christian*, to the Editor of which I am indebted for permission to reproduce them ın this form. They are now sent out, revised, with the prayer that both writer and readers may "go on" unto that spiritual ripeness of experience which alone realizes the divine purpose in Christ and fulfils the divine work of grace.

W. H. GRIFFITH THOMAS

CONTENTS

I.	INTRODUCTORY—A BOOK OF DOCTRINE....	7
II.	DIVINE REVELATION (Chap. 1:1-4).......	20
III.	"BETTER THAN ANGELS" (Chap. 1:5-14)...	25
IV.	THE PERIL OF DRIFTING (Chap. 2:1-4)....	29
V.	"NOT ANGELS, BUT MEN" (Chap. 2:5-18)..	32
VI.	"BETTER THAN MOSES" (Chap. 3:1-6)....	38
VII.	"LEST WE FORGET" (Chap. 3:7 to 4:2)....	43
VIII.	THE SABBATH OF THE SOUL (Chap. 4:3-13)	48
IX.	OUR GREAT HIGH PRIEST (Chap. 4:14-16)	53
X.	QUALIFICATIONS FOR PRIESTHOOD (Chap. 5:1-10)	62
XI.	DEGENERATION (Chap. 5:11-14)..........	67
XII.	EXHORTATION AND WARNING (Chap. 6:1-8)	70
XIII.	ENCOURAGEMENT (Chap. 6:9-20).........	76
XIV.	AN ETERNAL PRIESTHOOD (Chap. 7:1-10)..	81
XV.	A SPIRITUAL PRIESTHOOD (Chap. 7:11-19)..	86
XVI.	A PERPETUAL PRIESTHOOD (Chap. 7:20-25)	89
XVII.	PERFECT SALVATION (Chap. 7:25)........	92
XVIII.	A SUITABLE PRIESTHOOD (Chap. 7:26-28)..	97
XIX.	THE BETTER SANCTUARY (Chap. 8:1-6)....	100
XX.	THE NEW COVENANT (Chap. 8:7-13).....	104
XXI.	THE OLD AND THE NEW SANCTUARY (Chap. 9:1-10)................................	108
XXII.	A BETTER MINISTRY (Chap. 9:11-14).....	111
XXIII.	AN EFFICACIOUS MINISTRY (Chap. 9:15-22)	115
XXIV.	A COMPLETE MINISTRY (Chap. 9:23-28)...	119

Contents

XXV.	THE BETTER SACRIFICE (Chap. 10:1-10)	122
XXVI.	THE CROWNING PROOFS (Chap. 10:11-18)	126
XXVII.	APPROPRIATION (Chap. 10:19-25)	130
XXVIII.	"DO NOT DESPISE" (Chap. 10:26-39)	135
XXIX.	THE MEANING OF FAITH (Chap. 11:1-3)	140
XXX.	THE MANIFESTATIONS OF FAITH (Chap. 11:4-16)	143
XXXI.	THE DETERMINATION OF FAITH (Chap. 11:17-28)	147
XXXII.	THE DIFFICULTIES OF FAITH (Chap. 11:29-38)	152
XXXIII.	THE RACE (Chap. 12:1-2)	155
XXXIV.	THE CONTEST (Chap. 12:3-4)	158
XXXV.	THE TRAINING (Chap. 12:5-11)	160
XXXVI.	THE DUTY (Chap. 12:12-17)	162
XXXVII.	THE INSPIRATION (Chap. 12:18-24)	165
XXXVIII.	"DO NOT DEPART" (Chap. 12:25-29)	167
XXXIX.	IN INDIVIDUAL LIFE (Chap. 13:1-6)	172
XL.	IN SOCIAL LIFE (Chap. 13:7-14)	175
XLI.	CLOSING WORDS (Chap. 13:15-25)	179
	BIBLIOGRAPHY	185

"LET US GO ON"

THE SECRET OF CHRISTIAN PROGRESS IN THE EPISTLE TO THE HEBREWS

I

INTRODUCTORY

1. A BOOK OF DOCTRINE

THE EPISTLE to the Hebrews is undoubtedly one of the greatest and most important in the New Testament. Like Romans, Galatians, Ephesians, and Colossians, it is occupied largely with doctrine, though, as Romans and Galatians are concerned with the Work of Christ, Ephesians, Colossians, and Hebrews are mainly occupied with His Person. While the Epistle was addressed directly to Jewish Christians and its primary message was for them, it has a definite application to all believers, because of its special theme the fact and development of the believer's relation to God. Romans tells of coming out of bondage; Ephesians, of entering into the banqueting-house; Hebrews, of going up to the throne; First John, of abiding in the presence of God. Romans declares the divine righteousness which we are to receive; Ephesians, the divine fulness which we are to realize; Hebrews, the divine nearness in which we are to rejoice; First John, the divine oneness to which we are to respond.

2. AUTHORSHIP

From earliest days, Hebrews has been both ascribed, and also denied, to the Apostle Paul; and several other names have been suggested, including Luke, Apollos, Barnabas, Philip, and even Priscilla. But nothing is known of these names in connection with Hebrews; they are at the best personal opinions. One very interesting suggestion seems to deserve mention especially because it is favored by the great scholarship and spirituality of Franz Delitzsch. It is that the author is Luke— that it records Paul's thought in Luke's language. There are important words and phrases here which are only found elsewhere in Luke's Gospel and the Acts, and for this and other reasons Delitzsch holds that this Epistle is the third work of Luke in the New Testament. Godet says: "This Epistle, without introduction or subscription, is like the great High Priest of whom it treats, who was without beginning of days or end of years, abiding an High Priest continually. It is entirely fitting that this book should remain anonymous."

One thing is generally admitted: it was included in the New Testament, because it was originally thought to come from the Apostle Paul. At least, therefore, it can be called Pauline. According to a thoughtful and able Bible student, Mr. F. W. Grant, it would leave a serious gap in Paul's Epistles if Hebrews were taken away. He suggests, somewhat fancifully perhaps, that the Apostle's writings, though fourteen in number, form, according to their subjects, a double Pentateuch, the first series developing the Christian's position before God, and the second series developing our collective relationship to God. On this view the first series includes Romans, Galatians, Ephesians, Colossians (with Philemon), and Philippians. In the second are Thessalonians, Corinthians, Hebrews, Timothy, and Titus. This is certainly ingenious and also suggestive, especially in view of the fact that Hebrews would thereby be the third book of this "Pentateuch," corresponding to Leviticus in the Old Testament, with which, of course, it has many close points of contact.

In this connection mention must be made of two articles by Dr. Thirtle, which appeared in *The Christian* for April 27 and May 4, 1916, in which the endeavor was made to show that the Epistle to the Hebrews was originally intended for the Jewish Christians in the churches of Galatia, while the Epistle to the Galatians was intended for the Gentile Christians of that region. "Two epistles in close succession in a professedly Pauline section of the New Testament are merely separated or divided off the one from the other by the words 'to Hebrews.'" Hebrews was an "enclosure" and Galatians served as "covering letter" (see Gal. 6:11). Dr. Thirtle inferred that Paul wrote the document in Hebrew ("with mine own hand") and that Luke translated it into Greek. Thereupon he notices some striking parallels between the two Epistles. Thus, Hab. 2:4 is quoted in Gal. 3:11 and Heb. 10:38. Teaching on the Covenant is found in both Epistles (Gal. 3:15-17; Heb. 8 and 9). Both speak of Jerusalem which is "above" or "heavenly" (Gal. 4:26; Heb. 12:22), and both deal with "perfection" (Gal. 3:3; Heb. 6:1). This discussion is decidedly worthy of close attention by all students, because, even though it may not carry conviction, it suggests lines of thought that are eminently productive of valuable results.

3. Destination

The Epistle belongs to the Jewish Christian group of writings in the New Testament, like James and First Peter. It is clearly addressed to Hebrew Christians who were members of some definite community (13:7, 17-19, 22-24), and not to Hebrew Christians as a whole. Their needs are known to the writer, and there is a personal tone throughout (5:11, 12; 6:9, 10; 10:32-34; 12:4). The precise locality where these Hebrew believers lived is quite unknown, some thinking it was in Jerusalem, and others favoring Rome (13:23, 24). But whether they lived in Jerusalem or not, they still recognized the obligation of the Law, and were at least conversant with the Temple worship. Perhaps they had not yet fully perceived what was involved in Christianity, the abrogation of the Levitical sacrifices, and the transitoriness of the Temple services.

4. Date

It is generally thought that when the Epistle was written the Temple was still standing (8:4; 9:6; 12:27; 13:10), and the allusion to "the day approaching" (10:25), seems to indicate the catastrophe which happened in A.D. 70 in the destruction of Jerusalem. For these reasons it has been suggested that the date of writing is somewhere about A.D. 63-66.

5. Purpose

The Epistle was intended to lead these Jewish believers from a rudimentary to a mature knowledge of Christian truth. They had started well (6:10; 10:32-34), but had shown a tendency to pause on the journey, if not to go back (5:11, 12). They had not made progress, or striven after a fuller and deeper spiritual experience (6:1). For this reason thoroughness and steadfastness are shown to be essential. The two stages of the Christian life represented by babes and men are indicated (5:12-14), and the latter is seen to be the true realization of what the Christian life is intended to be. Perhaps this reluctance to go forward was strengthened by the fear of further persecution which seems to have been facing them (10:34). Several perils are pointed out, including dulness of spiritual perception, the possibility of spiritual degeneration (5:11-14), the danger of separating themselves from their fellow-Christians (10: 25), and the serious risk of being carried away by erroneous doctrines (13:9). And so the Epistle was written to lead from immaturity to maturity (6:1). "Let us go on" is, literally, "Let us be carried on." The safeguard against degeneration, isolation, and consequent failure is to make progress in the Christian life, and to proceed from point to point from an elementary to the richest, fullest, deepest experience.

6. PLAN

The purpose of the Epistle is carried out by means of an unfolding of the true nature of Christianity as the final and complete religion, beyond which there was nothing else to come. This is done by dwelling on the glory of the Person of Christ, and by contrasting the revelation of the Old Covenant with that of the New, with special reference to Priesthood. This Epistle is the only place in the New Testament where Christ is set forth as Priest. In other books He is seen to exercise priestly functions, but here He is a Priest. It is shown that the New Covenant is mediated by no less a Person than the Son of God. Two texts seem to sum up the Epistle: "Thou art my Son"; "Thou art a Priest," and in the full, deep knowledge of Him, in the glory of His Person and particularly in the power of His Priesthood, is to be found the means of growth, the spring of progress, and the safeguard against relapse, backsliding, and apostasy. What they needed was a deeper and truer meaning of Christ than they had hitherto obtained. Our Lord as Savior is regarded as applying to the commencement of the Christian life, while His Priesthood is thought of as connected with its continuance and permanence. Professor Nairne suggests that there is one theme running throughout the Epistle which is the key to its true meaning: "Think of Him as Priest and I will make you understand."

Certain key-words are found in the Epistle which help to a full appreciation of its purpose and plan. One of these is "Perfection," which, with its corresponding verb and adjective, occurs eleven times, and which (here as elsewhere in the New Testament) never means sinlessness. With one exception (13:21), it refers in this Epistle to a mature Christian experience, in contrast with a rudimentary one. A careful study of the various passages where this word occurs will give a clear idea of its meaning. Thus, it is said that law made nothing perfect (7:19), that is, spiritual maturity was impossible under the Old Covenant (7:11). But under the New Covenant this ripeness of experience is possible (6:1). Christ is described as the One through Whom this "perfection" is realized, because by His offering on Calvary (10:14), and His own personal life (12:1, 2), He has made it possible for His followers to realize it. We shall see as we proceed how wonderfully the Epistle teaches, as no other part of the New Testament does, the profound and blessed truth of the perfecting of

Christ (2:10; 5:8; 7:28). The more this idea of "perfection" is studied, the more it will be seen that the Epistle is intended to lead Christians forward into the completest and richest experience of living.

Another key-word is "Eternal," which is found several times (5:9; 6:2; 9:12, 14, 15; 13:20). There are also several phrases which have the same general meaning ("forever," 1:8; 5:6; 6:20; 7:17, 21, 24, 28; 13:8, Greek), and the idea in every case is of Christianity as an abiding and permanent religion in contrast with the temporary character of the Old Covenant.

A third key-word is "Heaven" or "Heavens" (1:10; 4:14; 7:26; 8:1; 9:24; 12:25, 26), with its adjective "Heavenly" (3:1; 6:4; 8:5; 9:23; 11:16; 12:22). Attention is thereby directed to the fact that the highest truths and deepest realities of the Christian faith and life are not earthly, or associated with a religion which, like Judaism, was solely concerned with an earthly sphere and with merely physical ceremonies.

A fourth key-word is "Better," which again is seen all through the Epistle in various connections. This expresses by contrast the superiority of Christianity to Judaism. Christ Himself is shown to be "better" than angels (1:4), and not only is He proved to be superior to the greatest names in the Old Covenant, but we read of a "better covenant," "better sacrifice," "better resurrection," as well as other aspects of the same fundamental truth.

Yet another key-word is "Partakers" (2:14; 3:1, 14; 6:4; 10:33; 12:8, 10), and its uses are very suggestive. In every case it means definite associations, companionship, or participation. Christians are thus one with Christ and their fellow-Christians, and the realities of Christianity are matters of actual experience, whether of joy or sorrow. Judaism could only symbolize and promise, but Christianity offers its blessings for definite, continuous, and permanent reception and enjoyment.

A sixth key-word is the phrase "having . . . let us" (4:14-16; 10:19-24). Corresponding with this, we have "leaving . . . let us" (6:1) and "we have" (8:1, etc.). All these suggest the absolute necessity and vital importance of appropriating what we possess, of making use of all that is ours in Christ.

In contrast with the last-named key-word there is one more to notice, the word "Lest" (2:1; 3:12, 13; 4:1; 12:14-16). It is expressive of the fear "lest" these great and glorious realities should after all be lost.

There seems to be a clear and close connection between these seven key-words. The complete realization of the Christian life is seen in the idea of "perfection" or maturity, and this is possible because Christianity is the "eternal" or permanent religion, and "heavenly" in character. As such it is something of which we can be actual "partakers," because Christianity is not a religion merely of *anticipation,* but of *participation.* As such it is "better" than, that is, superior to, Judaism, and because it is God's final word, we are to possess and enjoy it in order to realize all its blessings, and to watch carefully for fear we fall short of and fail to realize its priceless possibilities.

7. OUTLINE

While the Epistle as a whole is capable of detailed and elaborate analysis, its main lines can be stated in a very simple way, and a general analysis (apart from details) enables us to see clearly how the truths of our Lord's Person and Priesthood are presented for the purpose of emphasizing the need, duty, and privilege of Christian progress.

(1) Introduction. Chap. 1:14. The theme of the entire Epistle is seen here in germ. God's complete and final revelation is given in the Person (1:1) and Work (1:3) of Christ.

(2) The Supreme Glory of the Person of Christ as the Son of God. Chap. 1:5 to 4:13.

> (*a*) His Superiority to Angels, 1:5 to 2:18.
> > (Practical exhortation, 2:1-4.)
> (*b*) His Superiority to Moses, 3:1-6.
> > (Practical exhortation, 3:7 to 4:13.)

(3) The Supreme Glory of the Priesthood of Christ as Son of God. Chap. 4:14 to 10:18.

> (*a*) The Provision of the Priest, 4:14-16.
> (*b*) The Qualifications of the Priest, 5:1-10.
> > (Practical exhortation, 5:11 to 6:20.)
> (*c*) The Person of the Priest, 7:1-28.
> (*d*) The Work of the Priest, 8:1 to 10:18.

(4) The Personal Appropriation and Practical Application. Chap. 10:19 to 13:25.

> (*a*) The New Life, 10:19-25.
> > (Practical exhortation, 10:26-39.)
> (*b*) The First Encouragement to Progress, 11:1-40 (Faith).
> (*c*) Second Encouragement to Progress, 12:1-14 (Hope).
> > (Practical exhortation, 12:15-29.)
> (*d*) Third Encouragement to Progress, 13:1-17 (Love).
> > (Personal conclusion, 13:18-25.)

The above outline is compiled mainly from Westcott, Milligan, and Murray. The detailed plan of Murray's *The Holiest of All* is strongly recommended as accurate and helpful. Another helpful and suggestive outline will be found in *The Supreme Gospel,* by Kerr, pp. 17, 18, in which the entire Epistle is treated under the idea of the "supreme" things of which it speaks.

In this outline will be seen (inserted in brackets) at various stages five practical exhortations. They are a characteristic feature of the Epistle, being warnings interjected at each point of the treatment. They come in parenthetically, and the teaching of the Epistle can be considered apart from them because (though very important) they are merely pauses for exhortation and appeal. It has been suggested that these five parentheses are complete in themselves, and that there is a progress in their warnings. This is how the idea was stated in an interesting article which appeared some years ago in the *Christian Workers' Magazine,* of the Moody Bible Institute, Chicago, written by Rev. Robert Clark. Two things are to be noticed in each: the Biblical background and the sin against which we are warned:

Chapters	Background	The Sin
2:1-4	Sinai and Calvary	Neglect
3:7 to 4:13	Wilderness and Rest of God	Unbelief
5:11 to 6:20	Canaan and Fruits of Land	Apostasy
10:26-39	Sanctuary and Its Entrance	Wilful sin
12:15-29	New Jerusalem and Mount Zion	Obstinate refusal and indifference

These exhortations illustrate a well-known law of the human mind: Neglect will give place to unbelief,

unbelief to apostasy, apostasy to wilful sin, and wilful sin to indifference.

Their messages, as we shall see, can be summed up thus: "Don't drift"; "Don't disbelieve"; "Don't degenerate"; "Don't despise"; "Don't depart."

8. Value

Bishop Westcott, in his great Commentary, written sixty years ago, has these words: "The more I study the tendencies of the time in some of the busiest centers of English life, the more deeply I feel that the Spirit of God warns us of our most urgent civil and spiritual dangers through the prophecies of Jeremiah and the Epistle to the Hebrews. May our Nation and Church be enabled to learn the lessons which these books teach while there is still time to use them."

This general statement of the importance of the Epistle is as applicable today as it was to the time when it was first written, and the special truths needing to be emphasized are perhaps three in number:

(1) *The Person of Christ.*— In this Epistle, as perhaps nowhere else in the New Testament, both the Humanity and Deity of Christ are signally set forth. From the humiliation of earth, Christ is seen to be raised to exaltation at the right hand of God. When the Epistle says: "This is the sum" (8:1), or "This is the chief point" (R.V.), or, as Rotherham puts it, "This is the crowning-point," we see that the central theme of the Epistle is the exalted, Divine Lord Jesus Christ. As such He is superior to angels, prophets, and priests, and for the purpose of being our Redeemer, He is Prophet, Priest, and King. He is shown to be "God blessed for ever." As in the New Testament generally, so here, no idea of a mere humanitarian Christ is found. With

the strongest possible emphasis on His Manhood, there
is perhaps no place in the New Testament where His
essential Godhead is more unmistakably presented. This
Epistle puts Him in a place "in the eternal nature of
God, corresponding to His place in the temporal history
of man."

(2) *The Importance of Scripture as the Word of
God* is another truth clearly indicated in Hebrews. The
Old Testament is a divine revelation, even though
Christ is the supreme and final expression of God's
will and purpose for the world. It is particularly impressive to notice the use of Scripture in this Epistle.
The human authors are scarcely mentioned, everything
being traced primarily to God, Scripture being regarded
as emanating from Him.

(3) *The Christian Life is also Specially Emphasized.*—
Believers are reminded of the absolute necessity of
making progress, of growing in grace, and of not resting content with a superficial and elementary knowledge
of Christian truth (6:1). It is said that, before the discovery of America, Spanish coins which bore the im-
print of the Pillars of Hercules had a motto, *Ne plus
ultra,* "Nothing else beyond"; but after the success
of Columbus the motto was changed to *Plus ultra,*
"More beyond." So it is with the Christian life; whatever may be the heights to which the believer attains,
"still there's more to follow." This distinction between
the rudimentary and mature stages of the Christian life
is made by means of an emphasis on the Priesthood of
Christ. The vital question that faces every reader of
this Epistle is: What difference does it make to our
spiritual life between possessing Christ as our Savior
and our Priest? It is clear that, however it may be

explained, Christ's Priesthood is here set forth as the secret of progress and the guarantee against backsliding. It is this emphasis on the deeper, fuller aspects of the Christian life that makes the study of Hebrews so vital and important.

II

DIVINE REVELATION

(Chap. 1:1-4)

IN THESE four opening verses almost everything in the Epistle will be found in germ.

1. THE FACT OF A DIVINE REVELATION

There is no attempt to argue for the existence of God. The Bible never does this, but always takes it for granted (Gen. 1:1). Nor is there any discussion as to the possibility or even likelihood of a divine revelation. This is also presupposed and implied. "God has spoken." Revelation is, however, the opposite of discovery, and it is God who has revealed Himself, not man who has discovered God. Every believer in the existence of God necessarily believes that God can reveal Himself, and when it is remembered that "God is love," the probability of revelation becomes assured, since love must of necessity manifest itself. God's revelation is the vehicle, both of knowledge and of grace, of truth and of power. It calls for a response from man. "He that is of God heareth God's words."

2. THE REALITY OF THE OLD TESTAMENT AS A DIVINE REVELATION

"God having of old time spoken unto the fathers in the prophets by divers portions and in divers manners."

This plain statement shows that the Old Testament is at once real and yet incomplete as a divine revelation. God manifested His will through the prophets "by divers portions and in divers manners," which means fragmentarily and variously. Thus the Old Testament embodies a divine progressive revelation. This emphasis on the reality and yet the incompleteness of the Old Testament is of vital importance today, because it bears witness at once to the fact and also the limitations of that part of Holy Scripture.

3. THE SUPERIORITY OF CHRIST AS A DIVINE REVELATION

In marked contrast to the Old Testament, Christ is described as the One in Whom God has spoken "at the end of these days." Instead of a fragmentary, His is a complete revelation; instead of being temporary, it is permanent; instead of being preparatory, it is final; and instead of coming through subordinates, it is embodied in One Who is supreme. Thus the revelation in Christ is seen to be superior to the Old Testament in relation to character, time, destination, and Agent. While both the Old Testament and the New are divine revelations, there is at once continuity and contrast. The word "Son" is the central word here, and as the original has no definite article with the word, it suggests His character rather than His Person, *what* He is rather than *who* He is. His identification with the man "Jesus" will be seen hereafter (4:14); meanwhile, He is set forth, not as the instrument of God, but as God Himself speaking to us in a perfect revelation, which supersedes all others and meets all our needs.

The thought of Sonship is important, and calls for study all through the Epistle. There are no fewer than seven references to Christ as the Son (1:2, 5, 8; 3:6; 4:14; 5:8; 6:6; 7:28; 10:29).

4. THE PROOFS OF CHRIST'S SUPERIORITY

Immediately on speaking of the Son, the Epistle bursts out into a description of His glories. Instead of continuing by declaring what God has said in Him, a statement is made of Christ Himself as the One in Whom God has spoken. No fewer than seven things are said about Christ in proof of His superiority as the sphere and embodiment of the divine revelation (vv. 2-4).

(1) *Christ the Heir* (v. 2)—"Whom he appointed Heir of all things." This thought points forward to the end and crown of all history. Christ is appointed to inherit everything, and the heirship is of course with reference to His incarnate life and work.

(2) *Christ the Creator* (v. 2)—"Through whom also he made the worlds." The reference here is, not so much to the actual creation (John 1:2) as to the world as developed in time. "Through whom also he made the *ages*." The word is the same as in 11:3, and seems to refer to the plan and arrangement of the various dispensations through which the created world has passed, is passing, and will pass.

(3) *Christ the Revealer* (v. 3)—"Who being the effulgence of his glory, and the very image of his substance." As the first of the two former statements points onward to the end of history, and the second points backward to the beginning, so this goes further back still, and calls attention to Christ as He was before ever anything earthly existed. These two phrases describe Him in relation to God. He is the "effulgence" or "eradiated brightness" of God, and the "exact repre-

sentation of His very Being." The thought seems to be that as God's being was invisible, Christ, like the Shekinah glory, is the manifestation (or the exact expression) of what God is. Nothing could be more impressive as to the essential Deity of our Lord.

(4) *Christ the Sustainer* (v. 3)—"Upholding all things by the word of his power." He who was before history, at the beginning of history, and will be the end of history, is now seen to have a relation to the world all through history as its Sustainer and Upholder. The tense of the verb "upholding" is significant of Christ's constant work in relation to the world (Col. 1:17).

(5) *Christ the Redeemer* (v. 3)—"When he had made purification of sins." This is a new and much-needed thought, for the soul requires something more than the light suggested by what has been said in the four former declarations concerning Christ. He is not only the Revealer of God, but the Redeemer of man, and this particular aspect of His redemptive work, "purification of sins," is probably emphasized here because cleansing is the main theme of the Epistle. It is one effect of redemption, and seems to point back to the ceremonial defilement dealt with in the old law (Num. 19). It is also appropriate because, as the Epistle is for believers rather than for sinners, purification is naturally emphasized in this connection.

(6) *Christ the Ruler* (v. 3)—"Sat down on the right hand of the Majesty on high." The Lord having done His work, is seen to have obtained His rightful position (8:1; 13:20). It is significant that when the High Priest entered the Holy of Holies he did not sit down, no provision being made for this. But Christ, having accomplished His work of redemption, is shown by

this statement to have completed it—"sat down."

(7) *Christ Supreme* (v. 4)—"Having become by so much better than the angels, as He hath inherited a more excellent name than they." This superiority of Christ is shown by the fact that He is "Son" and not (as is an angel) a servant. As elsewhere, so here, the word "name" is the equivalent to nature. The thought is that Christ possesses the nature of God, as will be seen from the Old Testament in the following verses 5-14). As the result of His work of redemption, He has been "declared the Son of God with power" (Rom. 1:4).

Thus, in studying these verses, we see that Christ is all. He is prophet (v. 2); priest (v. 3); and king (v. 3). We have implied His Deity, His Incarnation, His Atonement, and His Ascension, and it shows why He could redeem mankind, and why He is essential for all believers. It is because He is uniquely related to God that He is able to be the Savior of men; and now, all that we need for the fullest, richest, deepest spiritual life is occupation with Christ.

III

"BETTER THAN ANGELS"

(Chap. 1:5-14)

THE STATEMENT of v. 4 that Christ is "better than the angels" is at once proved by means of a number of quotations from the Old Testament. It may be asked why so obvious a comparison should have been made, because to us there can be no question of the superiority of Christ to angels. But the Jews venerated angels because of their place in the giving of the Law (Acts 7:53; Gal. 3:19), and it was essential that Jewish Christians should learn by this comparison something of the infinite superiority of our Lord over those heavenly beings that held so prominent a place in Jewish life.[1] Those who accepted the Deity of Christ would of course have no need of this comparison, but the presentation of it from the standpoint of that Scripture which the Jew venerated would give special point to the theme of the Epistle in regard to the completeness and finality of the Christian religion. These quotations call for special study.

1. THE NUMBER

There are seven passages, all taken, with one exception from the Psalms. It has been well pointed

---

[1] A good presentation of the teaching of Scripture about angels will be found in *Better Things,* by Dr. J. Gregory Mantle, chap. II.

out (by F. W. Grant) that the series is "significant in this way, every text in its place, and the whole a sevenfold witness to the Lord in accordance with the doctrine in this Epistle." The passages are Ps. 2:7; II Sam. 7:14; Ps. 97:7 (see Deut. 32:43); Ps. 104:4; Ps. 45: 6, 7; Ps. 102:25-27; Ps. 110:1.

2. THE ORDER

It is probable that these seven passages are descriptive of Christ as "Son," from His Incarnation to His Glory. The first two refer to His Sonship; the third to His Coming; the fourth and fifth to His Exaltation and Rule; the sixth to His Millennial Reign, and the seventh to the Culmination of all things.

3. THE FORM

The first and second open with a question implying that no angel is ever addressed as "Son." The third calls upon the angels to worship the Son. Then comes a further comparison between the angels as servants and the Son as Divine (vv. 7, 8). Then follow further statements to prove the superiority and eternity of the Son (vv. 9-12). The whole passage is closed by asking whether any of the angels were ever told to sit on God's right hand (v. 13). The last question (v. 14) is a further indication that the angels do service, while the Son possesses divine authority. It is important to notice that the word "salvation" occurs here for the first time, and a careful study of its usage in this Epistle seems to suggest that it refers to believers rather than to those who have not yet accepted Christ as their Savior (1:14; 2:3, 10; 5:9; 6:9; 7:25; 9:28). It must never be forgotten that salvation covers past, present, and future, and deals with the penalty, the power, and the presence of sin. The main if not the sole thought in Hebrews is salvation in its fullest aspect, as involving the believer's complete redemption and full experience. A clear proof of this is suggested by the phrase, "inherit salvation," which points forward to something still to be possessed and enjoyed, instead of, as in the case of redemption, something already received (see I Pet. 1:5, 9). Then, too, the phrase, they "that shall inherit," is particularly important because of its meaning and usage in this Epistle and elsewhere in the New Testament. It implies a future that is certain, a salvation that is inevitable, so that we could render "those that are certain to inherit."

4. THE FORCE

It is very striking to study the form of the quotations here and throughout Hebrews. They are nearly all traced directly to God, and the human channel is not as a rule mentioned (3:7). Thus the quotations coming from writings regarded as sacred and divine, would carry the greatest possible weight with the Hebrew Christians to whom the Epistle was addressed. It is obvious that the Old Testament has a far deeper meaning than is often imagined in this present day. Here are passages which are beyond all question Messianic, referring to the divine source (v. 5), the divine worth (vv. 6-12), and the divine sovereignty (v. 13). The passages, while addressing the king, call Him God, and obviously this could not be true of any earthly monarch. It would be well for us if we could take the same attitude to the Old Testament as the writer of this Epistle, for it would yield a depth of meaning to which many have hitherto been strangers.

5. The Meaning

The one thought of all these passages is the superiority of the Son to angels. Such language as is here quoted was never used of angels. There seems to be a fivefold superiority: Sonship (v. 5); worship (v. 6); heirship (vv. 7-9); kingship (vv. 10-12); and rulership (vv. 13, 14).

6. The Message

The angels are seen to be inferior, both to the Son (vv. 5-13), and to the heirs of salvation (v. 14). The angels have a ministry that is real and yet limited. Many people seem to have the idea that angels occupy some place between man and God as intermediate, and this is doubtless true from one standpoint, but v. 14 appears to indicate that they are servants who minister to the people of God (I Cor. 6:3; I Pet. 1:12).

It is particularly noteworthy, as bearing on the main theme of the Epistle, that both Christ and Christians are described as heirs (1:2, 14). This is another proof that salvation, as here stated, refers in its fulness and completeness to the future for those who are the people of God.

IV

THE PERIL OF DRIFTING

(Chap. 2:1-4)

THIS IS the first of the five interjected warnings and appeals which are characteristic of this Epistle. After pointing out in chapter 1 that God has spoken in His Son (vv. 1-4), and that the Son is superior to the angels (vv. 5-14), this message concerning the need of listening to the Son is pressed home before further teaching is given, and He urges them to give heed to what they have heard. Under the figure of a drifting boat, the peril of indifference is indicated and the need of anchorage to the Son's revelation is pointed out.

1. THE NEED OF THE APPEAL

The readers are urged to give heed to things which they have heard, and to hold them fast with firmness. One of the greatest dangers of the Christian life is losing interest in what is familiar (8:9; Matt. 22:5). The entire Epistle lays stress on steadfastness at almost every stage, and this is one of the essential marks of the true, growing, deepening Christian life (3:14; 4:2, 12, 13; 6:1, 19; 10:26; 12:27, 28; 13:8).

2. THE BASIS OF THE APPEAL

In the word "therefore," reference is clearly made to what has preceded; the Divine Son and His final complete revelation (1:1, 2). Every application to the individual conscience must necessarily be founded on the importance and definite bearing of God's revelation.

3. THE URGENCY OF THE APPEAL

Although it is said "we ought," the original word means "we must," emphasizing a logical necessity, and giving as it were an irresistible argument, derived from the solemnity of the revelation made by Christ.

4 THE SOLEMNITY OF THE APPEAL

"Lest haply we drift away from them." This is a better rendering than the familiar words, "Lest at any time we should let them slip." The thought is of a boat being swept along past its anchorage with no oars and no sails, and at the mercy of currents. This is the seriousness of life, that with familiarity truths tend to lose their influence, and the result is an involuntary, gradual, and almost imperceptible backsliding, than which there is nothing sadder or more perilous in the believer's life.

5. THE REASON OF THE APPEAL

Once again a contrast is instituted between the two revelations (1:1, 2). The word spoken through angels in the old days (Acts 7:53; Gal. 3:19; Deut. 33:2) proved so steadfast that every transgression of the divine law received its righteous punishment; and since this was so, the responsibility becomes greater in view of the fact that now God's Word has come, not through angels, but "through the Lord," and has been confirmed through His servants who proclaimed it, while God Himself bore witness to this preaching by miraculous powers. The phrase, "so great salvation," is a striking reminder of what God has provided in Christ. The word "so" is similar to the instance in the familiar passage, "God so loved the world" (John 3:16), and expresses an unfathomable depth. The salvation is "great" because it is at once divine, free, full, sufficient, universal, and everlasting.

6. THE JUSTIFICATION OF THE APPEAL

"If we neglect." It is significant that there is no suggestion of rejection, but only of the risk of neglect. There are many who reject God's salvation, but there are very many more who neglect it because they find it so easy to drift. Someone has well put it in this way: "What must I do to be lost? Nothing!"

7. THE CONCLUSION OF THE APPEAL

"How shall we escape?" The obvious answer is that escape is absolutely impossible. As the old Welsh preacher once said, this question, "How shall we escape?" is one that no preacher or hearer, or even the wisest man on earth, can answer; indeed, neither the devil in hell nor God in heaven can answer it. Escape is impossible.

The protection against drifting is to have Christ at once the anchor and the rudder of life. The anchor will hold us to the truth, while the rudder will guide us by the truth.

V

"NOT ANGELS, BUT MEN"

(Chap. 2:5-18)

THE EPISTLE now reverts to the main line of teaching after the warning of vv. 1-4. Verse 5 is thus connected with 1:14, and the thought seems to be that it is not to angels but to men, in the representative man Christ Jesus, that God has subjected the coming habitable world. Thus the Son is better than the angels, not only as the revealer of God (chap. 1), but also, as will now be shown, as the representative of man. He has been made lower than the angels for a time with a view to the coming glory, when man will be restored to his rightful place in and through Christ. This thought of Christ as the representative man is seen in two ways.

1. THE PERSON OF THE REPRESENTATIVE MAN (vv. 5-9)

(1) The divine purpose for the world is that man, not angels, is to rule in the future. The "world to come" refers to the world in the future Messianic age, whether we call it millennial or eternal. This truth is supported from Psalm 8, and three things are mentioned in connection with God's purpose for human life. Man has been made a little lower than the angels; he has been crowned with glory and honor; and has been

set over the works of God's hands, with all things in subjection to him. This is what God originally intended for man, and it would have been realized but for human sin. Thus it is shown that Scripture says of man what it never says of any angel. Notwithstanding man's littleness, God intended his position to be one of remarkable greatness.

(2) But there has been delay in the realization of this purpose. Although everything has been subjected to man, "We see not yet all things subjected to him" (v. 8). Sin has entered, and robbed man of his dominion over everything else.

(3) And yet the divine purpose will be accomplished because, notwithstanding human sin, there is a divine plan for its complete realization (v. 9). We do not yet see man in authority, but we have the pledge and assurance of this glorious future for humanity in what Jesus Christ is and has done. We see "Jesus," and the name is appropriate because it is the name associated with His essential humanity. For a little time He has been made lower than the angels, in order that He might as man accomplish through redemption what God has purposed for human life. The original of v. 9, in its strict grammatical expression, teaches that Christ was crowned "for death," while in other passages we are told that He was crowned in or after death. What, then, are we to understand? Was He crowned before He died, or was He crowned because He had died? If the former—if He was crowned before He died— when did it take place? It has been suggested that the reference is to the Transfiguration (II Pet. 1:17), which was closely connected with His death, and could be described as a crowning in preparation for His suffering, giving merit to His death (Bruce, pp. 79-80). This

seems to be the only way in which the words "crowned for death" can be properly interpreted according to strict grammar. But elsewhere the crowning is clearly subsequent to the death (1:4; 12:2; Phil. 2:8, 9). This is, of course, true, though it does not express the literal phraseology of this verse, which speaks of our Lord's crowning "in order that" He should taste of death. The thought of our Lord's being crowned "for death," though undoubtedly novel, is very striking, suggesting that He was thus honored and glorified in preparation for Calvary.[1] Perhaps, however, in view of the strangeness of this thought, it might be well to accept both views, and think of our Lord as being twice "crowned," once before and for the purpose of dying, and then as the result and outcome of His sacrifice and humiliation. The idea of "tasting" seems to indicate a definite experience—not merely the fact of death, but the actual experience of what death is. He did not merely die, but entered into the full realization of its awful meaning and consequence. Thus, as the next verse says, He was "made perfect through sufferings."

2. THE WORK OF THE REPRESENTATIVE MAN
(vv. 10-18)

After the consideration of the Person, comes a statement of what the person does, and there are three aspects presented here.

(1) *In Relation to God—Its Fitness* (vv. 10-13).— God is described in His attitude to Christ, and the In-

[1] The Greek does not seem to be capable of any other rendering than: "because of the suffering of death, crowned (permanently) with glory and honor, in order that by the grace of God He might taste death for every man." This clearly states "crowned . . . in order that," and Rotherham, Govett, Nairne, and Holmes so interpret it. The discussions in the two first named are very weighty.

carnation is shown to be worthy of Him because the coming of Christ with His sufferings was based on the divine purpose and intention. On this account, it was not unfitting for Christ to die because He vindicated God by the purpose of His death. "It became him." The word "becoming" suggests the congruity of the sufferings of Christ with the divine intention, because they were for the purpose of "bringing many sons unto glory." The word "author" or "captain" means "leader," and is only found four times in Scripture—twice in this Epistle (12:2) and twice in Acts (3:15; 5:31). The word indicates one who is both prince and leader, and in the original there is a clear connection between the Leader and those whom He "leads" to glory. Once again comes the word "perfect," meaning the realization of an end or object. Christ was "perfected" in the sense of being equipped for His work as Savior, for obviously His Divine Person needed no perfecting. He was made perfect through sufferings, in order that He might accomplish His work of redemption. This oneness between leader and led is further emphasized in the following verses (11-13). The One who sanctifies and those who are being sanctified are essentially one, and for this cause Christ calls His followers "Brethren." The word "sanctification" in Hebrews is always associated with Christ, never with the Holy Spirit. Its meaning is consecration rather than purification; and it refers to position, not to condition (2:11; 9:12, 14; 10:9, 10, 14, 29; 13:12).

(2) *In Relation to Man—Its Necessity* (vv. 14-16).— Now comes the human side after the presentation of the divine (vv. 10-13). The Incarnation is seen to be real (v. 14), and its purpose is stated as being to "bring to naught him that had the power of death, that is, the

devil." Satan uses death to frighten God's children, but Christ through His death has robbed the devil of this power, for by dying He broke the association between sin and death. The subjects of the Incarnation are then shown to be not angels but men, the seed of Abraham. Here the Revised Version, not the Authorized Version, should be read. It is not that Christ has taken upon Him human flesh, though that is true, but that He takes hold of, in the sense of helping or undertaking, the cause of human nature. The specific reference to the "seed of Abraham" is a significant illustration of the primary Hebrew purpose and destination of the Epistle.

(3) *In Relation to Christ—Its Obligation* (vv. 17, 18).—After the work of redemption has been related to God and man, it is proper to call attention to its definite relation to Christ Himself. There was the obligation for Him to be made in all things like unto those whom He was to redeem, for the purpose of His becoming "a merciful and faithful High Priest in things pertaining to God, to make propitiation for the sins of the people." Christ is here called "Priest" for the first time, but it is only mentioned, the full treatment being deferred. It is a characteristic of this Epistle just to touch upon a truth, and then to dismiss it for a time, taking it up later for full treatment. The words "merciful and faithful" are important, because both are needed. Christ is at once "merciful" to man and "faithful" to God. The word "propitiation" is very important. It means "that which makes it consistent for God to pardon." It is sometimes said that propitiation in the New Testament is never directed to God, as though it were necessary to "propitiate" Him. But the question at once arises as to the real object of the word. How

could man be propitiated? There must be one who
propriates and another who is propriated; and when
the publican offered his prayer it was: "God be pro-
pitious to me a sinner" (Luke 18:13). The true idea
seems to be, as Dr. Forsyth has well put it, that God
offers to Himself the sacrifice of Christ, so that He
is at once the One who propitiates and the One who is
propitiated. This sets aside all idea of anything un-
worthy in God, like anger or offense, and refers to
His righteous attitude against sin. His justice could
not overlook sin and His love could not be indifferent
to the sinner, and so what His righteousness demanded,
His love provided (John 3:16), and Christ, God's gift
to the world, is "the propitiation for our sins." The
outcome of this work is stated in the last verse (v. 18),
in which it is shown that Christ had qualifications for
being High Priest, and on this account was able to
help those who are in need. He was tempted, and
in His temptation He suffered; and then, because He
shares our experiences of temptations, He is able to
succor them that are tempted. It is important to remember that there is no reference here to sin, but only
to the possibility of sin in temptation. Christ's ability
as stated here is one of several ways in which "He is
able" to accomplish all that we need. There are some
ten passages in the New Testament which declare that
Christ is "able," culminating in the assurance that "God
is able to make all grace abound" (II Cor. 9:8).

VI

"BETTER THAN MOSES"

(Chap. 3:1-6)

WE HAVE SEEN Christ in His superiority to angels as Son of God (chap. 1), and as Son of man (chap. 2); and now it naturally follows that He should be shown to be superior to the great Jewish law-giver, Moses, whose high position and reputation among the Jews required this proof of his inferiority to the Lord. The connection between this and the former suggestion perhaps is that as kinship (2:14-17) suggested priesthood (2:18), so priesthood implies a spiritual household, which in turn gives rise to the thoughts of service in the case of Moses and the builder of the house, God, and Christ the Son.

1. THE ADDRESS

The personal endearment ("brethren") by which this argument is prefaced is of special interest. The argument "wherefore" seems to be that because of Christ's sympathy and succor (2:17, 18), it is essential to realize the importance of the situation. The use of the term "brethren," signifying relationship, and the word "holy," indicating their position of consecration, naturally leads to the statement of their wonderful privilege, "partakers of a heavenly calling." There are two connected words in the New Testament descriptive of this privilege, one (as here) meaning participation (1:9; 2:14; 3:14), and the other meaning partnership (10:33). This "calling" is another indication of the object of the Epistle, suggesting the heavenly glory, present and future, to which the believer is summoned (2:7-10).

2. THE EXHORTATION

They are urged to "consider," that is, to observe closely, the Lord Jesus Christ, Who is here described as "Apostle and High Priest of our confession." They are not merely to occupy their minds with Him, though that, of course, is essential and important, but they are to "consider Him as faithful."

Already the High Priest has been described as "merciful and faithful," and now the latter of these two points is taken up, the former being deferred for later consideration. Christ is set forth as faithful to God, Who appointed Him as "Apostle and High Priest." When Christ is thus considered, the mind being concentrated on Him, the contemplation will inevitably lead to conduct, for thought is always intended to express itself in action, and if the soul is thus occupied with Christ, and He is given His right place, everything else will follow. The characteristic of Christianity is the place it assigns to Jesus Christ.

3. THE DESCRIPTION

Our Lord is here called "Apostle and High Priest . . . Jesus." The word "Jesus" is very scarce in the Epistles, but is found in Hebrews most frequently of all the Apostolic writings. It expresses the human and historical Person who appeared on earth, and is, therefore, to be distinguished carefully from the word "Christ," which represents the divine aspect of our

Lord. In view of the fact that the word "Jesus" is found almost invariably in the Gospels and very rarely in the Epistles, it can at once be seen that the latter usage is indicative of the humanity of Him who is "God over all, blessed forever." Every place in the Epistles where the word "Jesus" is found by itself calls for special attention as expressive of the earthly and human position, and it will be found that the argument often turns on the use of this word, any other being unsuitable to the particular thought indicated in the context (e.g., 2:9). The term "Apostle" is only used here of Christ, and seems to indicate that He was sent from (and by) God. It corresponds with the statement of the earliest verses (1:1, 2), and is pretty certainly analogous to the position and work of Moses as the divinely appointed prophet and messenger.[1] Corresponding with this, and complementary to it, is the term "High Priest," which is analogous to the thought of Christ as the Son of man (chap. 2). It expresses His relation to God as man's representative, and as such may be said to correspond with the position of Aaron the Priest. Thus the two titles complete our Lord's work as sent by God and as representing man. First comes the divine revelation, and then the human response. This is the second mention of priesthood (2:17), but the fuller treatment is once more deferred. "Our confession" has reference to a testimony that is at once clear and courageous. The same thought is found elsewhere in this Epistle, and should be carefully noted (4:14; 10:23; 11:13; 13:15; cf. I Tim. 6:12, 13). Confession of Christ in the New Testament invariably refers to our speech, our testimony in actual words, not (though this

[1] A good treatment of Christ as Apostle will be found in *God's Apostle and High Priest,* by Philip Mauro, pp. 14-50.

is true) to the witness of our life. The description of Christ as faithful appears to apply to the present time, not to His earthly life in the past, "as now being faithful." The faithfulness of Christ is the foundation of our strength and peace.

4. THE COMPARISON

Christ is compared with Moses in a twofold way. First, we see His superior glory, as the builder of the house has more glory than the house itself (1:2). Then there is superiority of position, as a son is higher than a servant. It is significant that in v. 1 our Lord is spoken of by His human name "Jesus," and in v. 6 by His Divine Name or title "Christ." The faithfulness of Moses refers specially to Numbers 12:7. The "house" is the community of Israel.

5. THE REMINDER

From this comparison between Christ and Moses the practical truth is at once indicated that Christ is "over His house," and that we have the privilege of being His house. The Hebrew believers would thus be shown that they possess in Christ something infinitely beyond what they had in Moses. And yet there was a reminder that this would not be fully realized unless there was faithfulness: "If we hold fast our boldness and the glorying of our hope firm unto the end." Freshness of spiritual enjoyment is only too apt to pass, and on this account it is essential to "hold fast" right to the end, especially because of the great future to which this Epistle constantly points forward. Weakness is a spiritual peril, and this emphasis on boldness and "glorying" is a significant reminder that only as we continue courageous and confident can we expect to be firm unto the end. There is an old saying about "whistling to keep up the courage," and there is no doubt that in things spiritual the secret of courageous and steadfast living is to be bold and to glory constantly in our Christian hope. Thus this thought of holding fast, found here and elsewhere (3:6; 3:14; 4:14), is another reminder that the Epistle is written for believers, and was intended to emphasize the need and duty of continued progress in Christian living. Only those can "hold fast" who have already "laid hold" of Christ (I Tim. 6:12, 19).

VII

"LEST WE FORGET"

(Chap. 3:7 to 4:2)

Now COMMENCES the second interjected warning which extends from 3:7 to 4:13. It is concerned with the peril of disbelief (see 2:1-4, the peril of drifting). After what has been said concerning faithfulness and continuance, the Christians are urged not to fall short of what God offers them. The "heavenly calling" (3:1) is seen to mean rest (3:11), and the appeal is an urgent one that they should not miss it. In v. 7 the psalm is quoted, "Today if ye shall hear his voice, harden not your hearts," and the long warning can be best understood in the light of this twofold appeal. The first part (3:7 to 4:2) is concerned with the thought "harden not your hearts," being an appeal to fear. This is followed by the entreaty to "Hear his voice" (4:3-13), making an appeal to hope.

1. AN EXAMPLE (vv. 7-11)

Israel in the wilderness is used as an example and illustration of believers at the present time. Just as Christ has been shown to be faithful (3:5, 6), so believers are urged by the solemn warning given to Israel to avoid faithlessness (3:12, 19; 4:2). They have the privilege of hearing God's voice (v. 7), but there is the sad possibility of hardening the heart, just as Israel

did, incurring God's displeasure and leading to the
solemn asseveration that they should not enter His rest.
The thought of rest here and throughout this section
is not that of relief from fatigue, but cessation from
work which has been well done.

2. THE WARNING (v. 12)

Once again there is the loving appeal to "brethren,"
and very tactfully the suggestion is given that they
might possibly ("lest haply") fail. The solicitude is
seen in the thought that even one might incur this
trouble, and through unbelief fall away from the living
God. This divine title is of supreme significance, and
shows that God's character is the same to believers as
to all else (3:12; 10:31; 11:22).

3. AN APPEAL (v. 13)

One of the best ways of keeping ourselves true is to
help other people, and the duty is here set forth of
exhorting one another. There is scarcely anything more
striking in Christian experience than the fact that in
helping others we often help ourselves.

> Is thy cruse of comfort failing?
> Rise and share it with a friend,
> And thro' all the years of famine
> It shall serve thee to the end.
>
> Love Divine will fill thy store-house,
> Or thy handful still renew;
> Scanty fare for one will often
> Make a royal feast for two.
>
> Lost and weary on the mountains,
> Wouldst thou sleep amidst the snow?
> Chafe that frozen form beside thee,
> And together both shall glow

Art thou wounded in life's battle?
Many stricken round thee moan;
Give to them thy precious ointment,
And that balm shall heal thine own.

The reason for this solemn exhortation is "lest any one of you be hardened by the deceitfulness of sin," and the word is pressed home by the thought of "day by day, so long as it is called Today." It is unfortunately one of the sad experiences of daily life that sin is so deceitful as to lead to hardness. As it has been well said, sin is like Jael, who, when asked by Sisera for water, brought forth milk, "butter in a lordly dish," but had the hammer and nail behind!

4. THE STATEMENT (vv. 14, 15)

Once more the believers are reminded of the need of patient continuance if they are to enjoy the fellowship of Christ. It is not enough to commence the Christian life; it must be continued "firm" unto the end. This does not mean the loss of salvation, but it undoubtedly signifies the certain loss of spiritual blessing if we are unfaithful, and do not "hold fast" the beginning of our confidence.

5. AN INQUIRY (vv. 16-18)

At this point it is important to read the Revised Version, when it will be found that there are three questions and three answers, the questions indicating so many stages of human sin and divine displeasure.

(1) "Who, having heard, provoked?" (v. 16). The answer is, the very people that were delivered from Egypt.

(2) "With whom was he sore vexed for forty years?"

(v. 17). The answer is, those who sinned and suffered the consequences.

(3) "To whom did he swear that they should not enter into his rest?" (v. 18). The answer is, those who had disobeyed. This word is very strong, meaning obstinacy as the result of unbelief (John 3:36). Here are three stages of the sinful attitude to God: provocation, v. 16; sinning, v. 17; obstinacy, 18. It must never be forgotten that this was sin by those who had been redeemed and were on the borders of Canaan.

This shows that a good beginning is not everything; for the influence of the world, with the "lusts of other things," carelessness and sluggishness, will lead even the believer into failure and sin. There is scarcely anything more solemn than the awful possibility of backsliding, especially as Scripture nowhere indicates how far astray a Christian may go or how long he may continue in this backsliding condition. The root of the trouble is undoubtedly the "evil heart of unbelief" (v. 12), which leads to a failure to make progress until it is too late.

6. AN EXPLANATION (v. 19)

The trouble in Israel's case has been seen to be unbelief. They were unwilling to take God at His word, and the result was that God could do nothing with them in the way of progress, and had to condemn them to nearly forty years' wandering in the wilderness. Whenever we do not believe God's Word, the inevitable result is that we doubt His power and love.

7. THE EXHORTATION (4:1, 2)

Now comes the application. We too are to "fear," lest like Israel we shall fall short of the fulness of divine blessing. God's promises are still open to faith.

As we shall see, true rest is available for those who are
ready to "trust and obey." We are not to treat Christ
as Israel treated Moses, or else we shall suffer in like
manner. Indeed, it will be worse for us, because the
good tidings which we have received are infinitely more
valuable than theirs. But the secret of the trouble in
both cases is the same. God's Word did not profit
Israel because there was no real faith in their lives.
According to the other reading, it means that the people
of Israel were not united by faith with those who, like
Caleb and Joshua, did hear and heed the Divine Word.
Faith is here shown to mean willingness to believe God's
ability to do what He says, and these two passages always need to be kept together: "With God all things
are possible"; "All things are possible to him that be-
lieveth."

As we review this solemn and searching passage, we
can see how the danger is to be met in the seven appeals
that are made: "consider" (3:1); "hear His voice" (v.
7); "harden not your hearts" (v. 8); "take heed" (v.
12); "exhort" (v. 13); "hold fast" (v. 14); "fear"
(4:1).

VIII

THE SABBATH OF THE SOUL

(Chap. 4:3-13)

THE WARNING is here continued and completed. We
are to "hear his voice" (3:7).

1. THE SPECIAL PRIVILEGE

The salvation already mentioned is here described
under the form of "rest," and it is shown that we who
believe actually do enter into rest (v. 3). It is interesting to observe the fivefold rest stated or implied in this
passage: creation rest; entrance into Canaan; the rest
of salvation (Matt. 11:27); the rest of consecration
(Matt. 11:30); the rest of heaven. But in this passage
the predominant thought is not rest of conscience
through redemption, but rest of heart through surrender
and obedience. The believer is regarded as already out
of Egypt and journeying toward Canaan. "The danger
is not lest the blood should not be on the lintel, but lest
we should break down by the way, as thousands did in
the wilderness . . . When he speaks of rest, it is the
rest of the kingdom he talks of, not the rest of the conscience" (*Musings on Hebrews,* by J. G. Bellett).

2. THE SIGNIFICANT CONFESSION (vv. 3-8)

It is shown that Creation did not exhaust the meaning of God's rest, because He spoke of a rest to Israel

by Moses long after Creation was finished. It is particularly interesting to notice the references to God's own rest, for it would seem almost, in this description of it, in connection with Canaan, that "My rest" includes the idea that God would have satisfaction in seeing His people enter fully into the enjoyment of the Promised Land. But even this did not take place, for verses 7, 8 go on to show that, when Israel entered into Canaan, they did not realize the entire rest purposed by God, because Ps. 95 dated from a time long after entrance into Canaan. More than this, the word "today," which is so emphatic, indicates that there is something still more to be expected and experienced in the way of rest (v. 8). It is important to notice that instead of "Jesus" in verse 8, we should read "Joshua," Jesus being the New Testament equivalent of the Old Testament word. And thus, as Jesus Christ has already been shown in His superiority to angels and Moses, so here He is stated to be superior to Joshua as the leader into rest.

3. The Special Explanation (vv. 9, 10)

The word "rest" is suddenly and it would seem significantly changed, and instead of the ordinary word, it means "Sabbath rest"; but the primary idea is concerned with the present and not with the future, with the believer's life here and now, and only with Heaven as the completing and culminating point, the thought of "the Sabbath of the soul" in fellowship with God. No doubt the future cannot be excluded, but we must take great care to concentrate attention on the present. It is a rest from striving, a rest through believing, and refers to the attitude of the soul toward God. "His resting place shall be glorious" (Isa. 11:10). This means not the absence of activity, but that harmony of soul within which produces loyalty of character and conduct; and just as God ceased working after Creation, so also, when we enter into spiritual rest, we cease from our striving, because, as our attitude is one of confidence in God, we are in harmony with His will. This is the Christian life, which we ought to enjoy, and it is this which, under the form of rest in this passage, is the great theme of the entire Epistle.

4. The Solemn Warning (v. 11)

Based on this gospel of rest for the soul, the believer is exhorted to give diligence to enter into it, "that no man fall after the same example of disobedience." By a striking paradox we are to strive to enter into rest, and this is another indication that the whole passage has reference mainly, and almost exclusively, to the need of the believer realizing to the full the present privileges and possibilities of his Christian position.

5. The Searching Admonition (vv. 12, 13)

The warning closes with a twofold reminder. First, about the "Word of God" (v. 12), and then about God Himself (v. 13). The Word of God is described as "living," because it comes from the living God; as "energetic," because of its powerful work; as "sharper than any twoedged sword"; as penetrating; and as discerning the "thoughts and intents of the heart." The word "sword" is thought by some to be better rendered by "knife," referring to the knife of the priest as he tested the lamb for sacrifice. The phrase "dividing of soul and spirit" suggests that the Word of God is so powerful that it can do what man's knife cannot do with the "joints and marrow." The phrase "quick to discern" is one word, "critic," the only place in the Bible where this term is found. It is significant that with all that is heard today about Biblical Criticism, the passage suggests the Word of God as the "critic," of our lives, and it is more than probable that if we allowed the Bible to "criticize" us more, we should "criticize" it a great deal less. Thus the warning is pointed by this solemn statement concerning the Word of God, which, as it has been well said, "wounds the sinner, condemns the hypocrite, and rebukes the saint." It is too perilous to trifle with the Word of God.

And this solemn and searching declaration concerning the Word is due to the fact that it expresses and represents God (v. 13), who is at once omniscient and our Judge. Every creature is manifest in His sight; everything is open before His eyes—"the eyes of Him to whom we must render an account" of our life.

In all this we see the vital importance of the warning against unbelief and the consequent necessity of true faith in the Word of God. It is not too much to say that the Bible as the Word of God is essential for every aspect of the spiritual life. It convicts of sin (Heb. 4:12); it converts the soul (Ps. 19:7); it cleanses the conscience (John 15:3); it consecrates the life (John 17:17); it corrects the wrong (II Tim. 3:16); it confirms the right (John 8:31); and it comforts and encourages the heart (Ps. 119:50, 54). The more, therefore, we can apply ourselves to the Bible, the better it will be for everything connected with our daily living. In particular, three things are essential: careful consideration; continual meditation; and close application. When it is said, "Thy word have I hid in mine heart" (Ps. 119:11), it means that the "heart" in Scripture is equivalent to what we term today "personality," which, as is well known, consists of the three modes of self-consciousness—mind, heart, and will. With the Bible in all three, as truth for the mind, love for the heart, and power for the will, the word of the Psalmist becomes true, "The law of his God is in his heart; none of his steps shall slide" (Ps. 37:31).

IX

OUR GREAT HIGH PRIEST

(Chap. 4:14-16)

AFTER THE long warning, 3:7 to 4:13, the Epistle now returns to its main point, Priesthood. Two hints have been given (2:17; 3:1), and now the subject is made clearer in 4:14 to 5:10, though it is not fully treated until chapters 7, 8, and 9. The High Priest has already been described as "merciful and faithful" (2:17). His character as "faithful" was shown in 3:1-6, and now the other aspect, "merciful," is indicated in 4:14 to 5:10. In 4:14 the thought of 3:6 (before the interjected warning) is taken up.

1. THE HIGH PRIEST IN RELATION TO US

He is called a "Great" High Priest, doubtless because of His Divine Nature (1:1, 2; 3:6). There is no real difference between a priest and a high priest, or rather, the difference was only one of degree and not of kind. Our Lord is sometimes called Priest, or as here "High Priest." Priesthood is not intended for the justification of the sinner, a truth which has to do with God as our Judge. Priesthood has reference solely to believers, and the special application made here is in view of our temptations.

It is important to distinguish between a Mediator, an Advocate, and a Priest. The Mediator reconciles God to man and man to God. The Advocate restores man after his sin. The Priest sustains man, and provides against his committing sin. The name of the Great High Priest is "Jesus, the Son of God," the name "Jesus" referring to His humanity, and suggesting nearness, oneness, and sympathy, and "Son of God" indicating His Deity, and suggesting power. Thus the Divine and the human are blended, after having been considered separately in chapters 1 and 2. This Great High Priest has "passed through the heavens," not merely to heaven, but through the lower heavens into the presence of God, and has entered into God's rest. This is a very important point, because it shows that Christ's Priesthood is exercised in heaven, not on earth. We shall see later on that the presence of a priesthood on earth would imply that atonement for sin had not been completely made, for, as it has been rightly said, "a priesthood on earth is an attempt to do over again what has been done once for all." It is this that makes the sphere of Christ's Priesthood in the heavens, that is, in God's presence, of such vital importance.

The character of the High Priest is stated in the words "touched with the feeling of our infirmities," though the negative form of statement, "We have not . . . who cannot" is curious, and would seem as though the truth had been denied. Or else it is put in this form for stronger emphasis. The point is that the divine glory of Christ's Priesthood is no barrier simply on account of His human experiences and sympathies. On the contrary, He has been tempted exactly as we are tempted, and the temptation has left a permanent experience behind it (Greek). But notwithstanding this temptation, Christ was "without sin." In the English and American Versions we read, "yet without sin," indicating the issue or result of the temptation. But, perhaps, the Greek is better when quite literally rendered, "apart from sin," expressive of the limitation of temptation. This means, if we omit the "yet," that Christ was tempted in every point like us, with the one exception of sin. Sin was not a temptation to Him because there was nothing in Him to respond to it, but it undoubtedly caused suffering, which was all the more intense because He was sinless.

This brings before us the remarkable and important point that Christ's sympathy is associated with His sinlessness. He feels with us because He is altogether unlike us. We might naturally expect the very opposite, and are perhaps sometimes inclined to think that Christ would be nearer to us if He were not a sinless being. But this idea is impossible, and even if it were not, it would be fatal. We must pay special attention to the word "infirmities," for Christ has no sympathy with our sins. The sympathy of sinfulness would be a weakness, since if Christ had not been victorious, there could be no assurance of victory for us. We should have to recognize the inevitableness of failure, for if He had not been victorious, there surely would be no hope for us. "To feel fully and truly with the tempted, it is not necessary to have fallen before temptation, but only to have endured it. He who resists until victorious, experiences the full force of the temptation, as he who yields does not. Sin deadens while holiness quickens sympathy even with the sinful" (Garvie, *Expository Times,* vol. 26, p. 547). As another writer well puts the truth: "It is the love which suffers, not the weakness which fails, that is able to help us" (Whitham).

The matter is so vital that it is essential for us to be quite clear on this point of the necessary connection between Christ's sinlessness and His sympathy. "The sinner is an ill judge of sin; there will be undue abhorrence, or mawkish sentiment, or carelessness. A clear, uncolored view is needed." Another writer remarks, that "it is not necessary that He should have Himself succumbed . . . in order that He should know . . . One knows the sin and the death which one has 'perfectly met and overcome, better than if one had in the least been overcome by them" (Du Bose, *High Priesthood and Sacrifice,* p. 150). A friend has called my attention to the fact that, long ago, Plato expressed the same idea when he remarked that the best doctor is the man whose knowledge, not whose experience, of bodily ills is the greatest. In the same way, he says, a judge is the most capable of knowing and judging guilt if he is himself free from the evil habits, and qualified by personal excellence to administer justice. It is not the smart judge who is guilty of crimes himself that can best deal with the crimes of others. "The problem was to secure sympathy and yet to preserve sinlessness. The solution is found in temptation of the severest kind met by perfect resistance. And the keenest agony of temptation can be known only by one who remains sinless. Others are tried till they yield, and those who yield soonest suffer least . . . All our temptations Christ knew, feeling them, not with our coarse and blunted perceptions, but with exquisite and fine-strung sensitiveness . . . Sinlessness alone can truly estimate sin, for the very act of sinning disturbs the balance of the moral judgment" (*Century Bible,* p. 130).

It will be seen from this, that so far from our Lord's sinlessness making His temptation unreal, the truth is exactly opposite, for it is because of His sinlessness that He felt the temptation most acutely. A person who has been all his life accustomed to moral evil is far less likely to realize its hideousness than one who has always been surrounded by purity, and has had no experience of vice and degradation.

This question of the sinlessness of Christ and yet of the reality of His temptations is of such supreme importance that it calls for thorough attention. We must carefully distinguish between testing and tempting (Jas. 1:2, 14; Gen. 22:1). Christ was tested but never enticed, because there was nothing in Him to respond to sin. He had our human weaknesses but not our sins. Weakness to us is often the occasion of sin, but while He felt our weakness, He was not led thereby into sin. "Not only is Christ's sinlessness true of Scripture, but evidently also He was totally immune from the sense of sin, free from all inward discord or imperfection or discontent with self. Yet this is no automatic or effortless condition. His sinlessness (from the human standpoint) stands in the perfect fidelity to the Father of a will exercised under human conditions, filled absolutely with the Holy Spirit willingly received" (Bishop Moule, *International Bible Encyclopedia*, art. "Sinlessness").

The impossibility of sin in Christ is exactly the same as the impossibility of falsehood in God (Tit. 1:2). While therefore His temptations were real, yet not for a moment even in thought did He yield, nor was there any wavering in His perfect holiness. He could not sin because He would not. Some one has remarked that "the nature of Christ's temptations was determined by His unique vocation. Lower passions never assaulted Him." We may say, for example, that temptation to theft does not affect us in the least, because we are not assailable at that point. Now what we are at any one point, Christ was at all points. His integrity was unassailable. "He could have sinned if He had willed, but it was impossible for Him to will to sin." Dr. Plummer suggestively points out that: "The force of a temptation depends, not upon the sin in what is proposed, but upon the advantage connected with it. And a righteous man whose will never falters for a moment may feel the attractiveness of the advantage more keenly than the weak man who succumbs; for the latter probably gave way before he recognized the whole of the attractiveness; or his nature may be less capable of such recognition. In this way, the sinlessness of Jesus augments His capacity for sympathy: for in every case He felt the full force of temptation" (Luke 4:1-14).

It is also essential to remember that temptation does not arise only in connection with the sinful nature, for we have certain natural desires which are "morally neutral, and become sinful only when they are seen to be in conflict with the will of God." We are apt to overlook the fact that the devil does not tempt the sinful element in us, which is already on his side, and needs no evil solicitation. It is the better part of our nature that he endeavors to drag down into sin, and on this account "it was the fixed and righteous will of the Lord Jesus which the adversary tried to deceive, corrupt, and overthrow." [1]

---

[1] "The question therefore arises: Can one whose human nature was both without any hereditary taint and also from its union with the divine nature necessarily incapable of sin, be said to have endured real temptation, or to have been 'in all points tempted like as we are'? The answer seems to be that only he has felt the full force of temptation who has never yielded to it. Against Him who stood firm the whole conceivable power of temptation was exerted. He experienced it at all points. The fact that through the union

We must, therefore, guard carefully against two extremes. The one is that Christ could not be tempted if it were impossible for Him to sin; the other, that His temptation was not real, and therefore, His humanity is of no value to us. His temptations were unmistakably real, and it is just because of His absolute sinlessness that His humanity is of the most precious spiritual value for us.

2. OUR RELATION TO THE HIGH PRIEST

The message is clear that because the High Priest is all that has been indicated, we are to make use of Him for our individual needs day by day.

(1) There should be the consciousness of spiritual possession; "having then a great High Priest." This thought of "having" is characteristic of the Epistle, as we have already seen, and it implies a present reality in things spiritual. By means of this the Jewish believer would be reminded that all the old blessings of his religion really remained, and were uplifted and intensified by this present experience of "Jesus, the Son of God," the human and Divine Priest. Westcott somewhere

of the two natures it was impossible for Him to yield takes nothing either from the force of the temptation which attacked Him or from the completeness of His knowledge of it. To take a simple illustration: a breakwater conceivably might be so constructed that it would be impossible for the sea to break it. Such would endure the utmost power of the waves, whilst a weaker one might succumb before the full force had been felt. No doubt a moral example is more complete when it is set by one who, in every respect, is under exactly the same moral circumstances as ourselves. But had Christ come, not merely 'in the *likeness* of sinful flesh' but in flesh that was actually tainted with original sin, He could neither have been our Redeemer nor a perfect model of humanity. Nor does the truth that Christ was incapable of sin impair His moral liberty. God is the one Being who is perfectly free, but God cannot sin. Liberty in its highest sense does not carry with it the capacity of doing evil" (Holmes, p. 191).

points out that the word "have" always means conscious possession and not merely the fact.

(2) There must also be spiritual persistence, "Let us hold fast our confession." The "confession," as elsewhere (3:1) means the heavenly calling, courageously expressed as our own. To this we are to "hold fast," to keep clinging to it, and never to give it up.

(3) There is also to be spiritual freedom, "Let us therefore draw near with boldness." This term "draw near" is found here for the first time, and expresses our attitude of worshipful approach to God (7:25; 10:1-22; 11:6, Greek). The present tense is singularly significant, "Let us therefore keep on drawing near." In Bruce's words, "Christianity is a religion of access."

(4) The first result of this drawing near will be mercy; "that we may receive mercy." This is mentioned at the outset because of sin, for mercy is our primary need. The phrase, "throne of grace," is interesting, especially when compared with the other thrones mentioned in Scripture, "throne of judgment"; "throne of majesty"; "throne of glory"; "throne of iniquity." St. Paul elsewhere speaks of grace reigning (Rom. 5:21).

(5) The next result in our life will be "grace"; "find grace to help in time of need." It is interesting, whatever may be the meaning, to notice that we receive or "take" mercy, while we "find" grace. This is something like our Lord giving us rest and our finding rest (Matt. 11:28-30). As we need mercy because of our sin, so we need grace because of our weakness. The root of the latter word suggests a cry by reason of some calamity, and on this account it is implied that we need succor to avert trouble, "for seasonable help." Grace is the greatest word of the Bible because more than any other it expresses the essential character of

Christianity. One of the best definitions is "the love of God in active exercise on behalf of sinful men" (J. K. Mozley), and the three parts of this definition should be noted. Grace is God's love, that is, His attitude; it is God's love in exercise, that is, His activity; and it is God's love exercised toward men who are sinners.

As we ponder these wonderful verses, we notice that Christ as our High Priest has obtained for us access to and acceptance with God, and on this account we may and must be courageous in our confession. But He also possesses sympathy, and on this account we must and should have confidence in approaching Him. His greatness inspires our courage, and His sympathy elicits our confidence.

X

QUALIFICATIONS FOR PRIESTHOOD

(Chap. 5:1-10)

THE CONNECTION between this and the foregoing paragraph is clearly indicated ' by the word "for." Now comes the confirmation of 4:14-16, by showing what true priesthood is and what it requires. It means oneness with man (vv. 1-3) and authority from God (v. 4), and then it is seen that Christ has both of these (vv. 5-8), and on this account is Priest and Savior (vv. 9, 10).

1. THE ESSENTIALS OF PRIESTHOOD

Two qualifications were necessary to make a man a priest.

(1) Fellowship with man (vv. 1-3). This gives the essential definition of a priest. He is "taken from among men," and is "appointed for men in things pertaining to God," the "things" being gifts and sacrifices for sins. But more than this, the true priest is one who has sympathy with men because of their weakness and sin, "Who can bear gently with the ignorant and erring, feeling he himself also is compassed with infirmity." The word for "bear gently" is very interesting and suggestive. It means one "who can have a moderated feel-

ing," one who is neither too lenient nor too severe, because he knows what weakness is. On account of his own sin, as also because of the sins of the people, the priest is necessarily compelled to offer sacrifice (v. 3).

(2) Authority from God (v. 4). Not only must the priest have the human qualifications already mentioned, he must be able to show divine authority as well. He is not self-elected, for no one who realized his need of such qualifications as are stated in verse 2 would think of taking upon him the office unless he were appointed by God.

2. THE ESSENTIALS OF PRIESTHOOD FULFILLED IN CHRIST

We shall now see how Christ meets these two vital necessities, fellowship with man and authority from God, but the order is exactly reversed.

(1) Christ was divinely appointed (vv. 5, 6). His priesthood is based on His Sonship, the latter truth being the theme of chapter 1. And because He is Son, He is, therefore, Priest, and has been appointed by God.

(2) Christ also had fellowship with man (vv. 7, 8, 9a). His human life is mentioned, "the days of his flesh," and His human needs are indicated in the fact of His prayers. The intensity of His supplications is also seen, "prayers and supplications with strong crying and tears unto him that was able to save him from death." This seems a clear reference to the story of Gethsemane, and the phrase literally is, "save him out of death," which shows that He did not pray to be saved from dying, but saved "out of death" through resurrection. Some think that the prayer was to be saved from premature dying in the garden, lest through Satanic

power over His frail body He should not reach the cross. But this does not seem quite so natural and obvious as the idea of a prayer to be saved from all that death meant, by means of the issue of a joyous resurrection.

But whatever the prayer was, it was answered, for we are told He was "heard for His godly fear," or, as Alford well puts it, "by reason of His reverent submission." The result of these experiences was human discipline (v. 8). "Though he was a Son, yet learned he obedience by the things which he suffered." This does not mean for an instant that there was anything like disobedience or even the slightest tendency toward a difference between His will and that of the Father. His attitude of obedience was perfect from the first, "Lo, I come to do Thy will, O God." But by means of His experience of human life the attitude of obedience was expressed in action. And so it was not that He was learning to obey as though there was any opposition of will, but was learning obedience by means of discipline. This is the difference between innocence and virtue. Innocence is life untested, but virtue is innocence tested and triumphant. Thus Christ fulfils completely the twofold requirement for priesthood.

3. CHRIST'S PRIESTHOOD

By means of this discipline Christ was made "perfect," that is, mature, ripe, fitted for His work, and because of this fitness He became unto all them that obey Him the author of eternal salvation. Salvation is again seen to be wide and all-inclusive, covering past, present, and future, and of this "eternal salvation" Christ is the author or cause, just as in 2:10 He is called the "leader," or "pioneer." It is also noteworthy that this salvation is dependent on His priesthood, thereby showing once more that salvation in this Epistle refers to the believer and not to the unconverted. Salvation to the sinner comes through Christ as Savior, while to the believer it comes through Christ as Priest. The same idea is seen in the word "obey," for, while the sinner is saved through faith, it is in loyal, constant, faithful obedience that believers realize and enjoy that continuous salvation which will find its culmination hereafter.

As we review these verses we can see in verse 7 the school in which Christ was taught; in verse 8 the lesson He learned; and in verse 9 the result. Our Lord went into the school of suffering, learned the lesson of discipline, and because thereby He came to understand us thoroughly, He became our Savior, and as such was "designated" or "greeted" of God a High Priest after the order of Melchizedek. The Epistle lays great stress on the discipline of suffering experienced by Jesus Christ as the condition of fitness to be our Savior (2:9, 10, 14, 17; 4:15, 16; 5:7-9; 12:2).

Note Well—It is important to have a clear idea as to what constitutes the essential difference between a prophet and a priest. A prophet is one who represents God to man, a spokesman for God (Exod. 7:1 gives an exact illustration). A priest is one who represents man to God (as Heb. 5:1, 2 shows). Everything else done by either prophet or priest was no necessary part of the office. Thus, though a priest blessed others (Num. 6:23), blessing was associated also with patriarchs, prophets (Gen. 47:10; Exod. 39:43; Deut. 33:1; Josh. 22:6), leaders and kings (II Sam. 6:20; I Kings 8:14, 55). But there were certain functions which only a priest could perform, as may be seen from the story of Uzziah (II Chron. 26:18). When this distinction between prophet and priest is understood, the term "priestly absolution" is at once seen to be a contradiction in terms, because (1) absolution (meaning, as it does, something coming from God to man) is the work of a prophet, and (2) the Jewish priests never absolved. The Old Testament will be searched in vain for a single instance of a priest forgiving or absolving from sin. The careful distinction between prophet and priest is thus of great service today in the face of sacerdotal claims to absolution. It also enables us to understand why Christian ministers are never called priests in the New Testament. They do not, because they cannot, represent man to God. But ministers are called prophets because they can and do represent God to man.

XI

DEGENERATION

(Chap. 5:11-14)

AT THIS POINT comes the third interjected warning, which is graver than the former two. It is on the peril of spiritual degeneration. The teaching on priesthood about to be given had to be checked owing to the difficulty which the writer felt. But this was in the hearers rather than in the subject, for although the special theme was hard to be understood, the lack of progress in the hearers had led to weakness of spiritual understanding. Yet a careful study of the previous references to priesthood will show a definite progress of thought (2:17; 3:1; 4:14-16) which, in spite of the enforced digression, prepares for the full treatment in 7:1 to 10:18.

1. THE PROBLEM (v. 11)

There were many things to be said concerning the priesthood after the order of Melchizedek, but it was difficult to explain the matter to them, since the trouble was with them and not with the subject.

2. THE EXPLANATION

They lacked "push and go," they had become sluggish (6:12) in their capacity for listening to the truth.

There had been degeneration ("become") and through neglect they had gone back. There was "a languid indolence of mind and body" (Holmes). The words "dull of hearing" represent the same original term as is translated "slothful" in 6:12. Spiritual degeneration is therefore possible because God's will for the believer is constant progress.

3. THE REBUKE (v. 12)

In view of the time since their conversion, they ought to have become instructors of others, instead of which they were themselves still in the elementary class, needing to be taught. When a man has been a Christian for a long time, he ought to be giving instead of receiving help from others.

4. THE REMINDER (vv. 13, 14)

Under the figure of a babe they are told what they were in regard to spiritual capacity, unable to digest solid food and compelled to live only on milk. This shows the sinfulness of degeneration; because, while remaining "babes," they were without skill in the way of divine righteousness. Spiritual babyhood is natural and beautiful directly after conversion (I Pet. 2:1, 2), but just as it would be in things physical if a person's development was arrested, and he continued a babe in body and mind for several years, so it is in things spiritual—the spiritual charm of the babe in Christ becomes the very opposite of beautiful if the believer remains a "babe" for years. The New Testament frequently emphasizes this difference between the spiritual babe and the spiritual adult, pointing out both the admirable and also the regrettable features (I Cor. 2:6; 3:1; 14:20; Eph. 4:13, 14). One of the most important features of maturity as distinct from immaturity is a capacity for spiritual perception and skill in spiritual discernment. Elementary truths are essential for those who have just commenced the Christian life, but it is altogether different when a person has been a Christian for years.

5. POSSIBILITY (v. 14)

It is a great satisfaction to realize that spiritual degeneration, though sinful and harmful, is also remediable. These Christians, though "without experience," might still, "by reason of use, have their senses exercised to discern good and evil." There is a spiritual discrimination possible with a mature experience, and this can be the privileged possession of every believer (Isa. 7:16; Deut. 1:39).

From all this, it is easy to see the perils of stationariness and the sad results of spiritual dulness. Degeneration is harmful to ourselves and others, for one principle of the Christian life is "use or lose." A great pianist once said that if he ceased practicing for one day, he realized the loss; if he ceased for two days, his friends became conscious of it; while if he ceased for three days, the public quickly recognized it. The supreme necessity, therefore, is the "use" of our spiritual "senses," in order that, through constant exercise, we may "grow in grace, and in the knowledge of our Lord and Saviour Jesus Christ" (II Pet. 3:18).

XII

EXHORTATION AND WARNING

(Chap. 6:1-8)

AT THIS POINT the rebuke develops into an exhortation
to cease being spiritual babes, and to go on unto a
ripe experience. The exhortation, "Let us go on"
(Greek, *pherōmetha*) is particularly appropriate and
forcible at this point.[1]

1. THE NEED OF PROGRESS (vv. 1-3)

The alphabet seems to refer to Judaism[2] as expressive
of a time of spiritual infancy, and its elementary principles are to be left in the sense that we always "leave"
our elementary knowledge when we proceed to higher
and fuller attainments. We assume the alphabet as a
foundation, but do not think of remaining there, for

---

[1] I cannot forbear quoting here one of Dr. Alexander Smellie's
felicitous comments: "There never was a finer instrument of expression
than the Greek of the New Testament. It can pack so much into
a single word. This *'Pherōmetha'* is an instance. The Authorized
Version renders it, *Let us go on.* The Revised Version renders it,
Let us press on. Bishop Westcott, in his commentary on the Epistle,
prefers to render it, *Let us be borne on.* The truth is that it needs
all three to disclose the verb's significance and wealth. Put them
together, and they speak to us of three dangers which beset us as
we look to the perfection in front. There is the danger of sinking
into discouragement. And there is the danger of supposing that we
are left alone."

[2] See Ridout's *Hebrews*, p. 99: "The period of infancy is Judaism,
and the period of manhood is Christianity."

we could not possibly waste our time by continuing
to work at the foundation. A building must be erected
thereon (v. 1). The question arises whether there are
six or four things mentioned in verses 1 and 2. Most
writers regard them as six in number, consisting of
three pairs, the first pair referring to our personal relation to God, the second being concerned with our
corporate relation to others and to society, and the third
dealing with our attitude to the future life. But there
is something to be said for the view that there are
only four points mentioned, the' phrase "the doctrine
of baptisms and of laying on of hands" being put in
brackets as expressive of the spiritual interpretation of
the former two points, repentance and faith. On this
view, the passage would read thus: "Not laying again
the foundation of repentance and faith (that is, the
teaching [or meaning] of baptisms and laying on of
hands) and resurrection of the dead and eternal judgment." It is certainly strange that such ideas as "baptisms" and the "laying on of hands" should be put on
a level with the other four. Moreover, it is profoundly
significant to observe how little distinctively Christian
there is in this statement. Repentance, faith, resurrection, and judgment were certainly Jewish, and on this
account the reference seems to be to the Jewish foundation, and they are urged to avoid these elementary
things which they are to leave for something higher
and richer. Another reason for thinking these elements
are Jewish, not Christian, is that the word "baptisms"
is in the plural, and is also not the one that is ever
found elsewhere to describe Christian baptism. The
term, therefore, appears to refer to Jewish "washings."
It is also true that the "laying on of hands" was Jewish,
for we know it was connected with the work of the

High Priest on the Day of Atonement. It hardly seems possible from the Christian standpoint that ordinances like baptism and the laying on of hands can be put in the same category with the other four, which are spiritual realities, and on this account the Jewish interpretation appears best, especially when it is remembered that the Epistle is written to Jewish Christians.

The meaning of "This will we do, if God permit" or "Let us do this if God permit" (v. 3) is difficult. It only can mean one of two things. "This will we do" may mean either "this going forward" (we will do) or "this dealing again with elementary principles." Some writers think that the Epistle does deal with this again in chapter 10, but while this view is not so natural as the other, the reference to a divine "permission" for going forward is hard to understand.

2. The Solemn Warning (vv. 4-8)

Then follows one of the most serious warnings found in the Epistle, and one that has caused a great deal of difference of opinion. It may help us to understand its meaning if we take the general idea first, and bear in mind that its primary interpretation must be in strict relation to what has preceded, and to the particular circumstances against which the Apostle is writing. These Christians are to go forward, "for" (v. 4) it is impossible to restore those who through continued spiritual babyhood fall away. The description of these people must be noticed. They were "once for all enlightened." They had "tasted of the heavenly gift." They had been "partakers of the Holy Spirit." They had "tasted" the Word of God and the spiritual world. These four statements clearly imply a real and definite spiritual experience. It does not seem possible to interpret these phrases of illumination only, of light rather than of life.

Then comes the question of the fall: "If they shall fall away." The thought must be strictly limited to the text and not made general. It is no ordinary or general fall, but a deliberate apostasy, not backsliding but wilful departure. Practically everything turns on the force of the word "impossible" which, of course, must not be in any way weakened. It is absolute and unqualified. Whoever may be referred to here, it is "impossible" to restore them. This fact alone shows clearly that the passage cannot refer to ordinary backsliding from which restoration is, of course, possible. But does it mean impossible to man or to God? Some think that the reference is to human agency only, implying that man can do nothing with apostasy, which must be left with God. As it is no question of mere relapse but a definite turning aside, it is obviously impossible for the Christian community to restore such a wilful state. But it is best to take it just as it stands and interpret it of impossibility in every respect. The explanation of this impossibility is seen in verse 6, where there is a significant change of tenses. It is pointed out that it is unfortunately possible to "keep on crucifying Christ afresh," that is, after they have fallen, and on this account it is impossible to "keep on renewing them to repentance." Active hostility to Christ ever persisted in cannot be a matter of restoration, though, of course, as it has often been pointed out, if the cause ceases to operate, the effect will cease to follow. (See Edwards' *Expositor's Bible,* Hebrews, p. 94 note.)

There seems to be no doubt that this section is not concerned with mere professors of Christianity, since every prominent word used is found applied to believers in other parts of the New Testament. The word "once" means not to be repeated, as in 9:7, 26, 27, 28, while "enlightened" is the same as in 10:32, "partakers" as in 3:1, and "tasted" as in 2:9. Moreover, a mere professor of Christianity could not go on to maturity when he had not really started, nor could salvation in the elementary sense be denied to such a person. Then, too, a professor would not be warned, since he had never possessed grace. The passage is apparently a supposed case to correct their wrong ideas, and the argument seems to be that if it were possible for those who have had the experience of verses 4-6 to fall away, it would be impossible to renew them unless Christ died a second time, and this would put Him to an open shame and prove that His work was not of infinite value. It would be going back to that Judaism which brought about the crucifixion. Another point in favor of this interpretation is that the supposed case is spoken of in the third person, "those," "they," "them," while later on (v. 9) the direct personal address is resumed, and it is shown that these solemn warnings were not contemplated in connection with the readers' own lives. The real trouble was that they were spiritual babes when they ought to have been adults, and the exhortation preceding this warning is, as we have seen, to leave the elementary truths and avoid spending all the time in first principles.[3]

[3] Of all the various interpretations of the passage which I have read, this appears to me the most satisfactory. No true exegesis is possible which does not take fully into consideration four points: (1) The context ("for," v. 4) which limits the idea strictly to the need of progress from immaturity to maturity, from the elementary religion of Judaism to the final religion of Christianity; (2) The force of the word "impossible," which as it is absolute, can only refer to deliberate apostasy and not to backsliding; (3) The fivefold description of spiritual experience in verses 4 and 5, which cannot fairly be applied

The warning is followed and pointed by an illustration from the soil (vv. 7, 8). On the one hand, the earth receives rain, produces fruit, and obtains blessing; on the other, there is a production of thorns, with rejection and burning at the end. This seems to indicate that Nature proves the truth of persistence in one course as leading inevitably to one end. "Understanding of the higher truths is God's blessing on goodness, and destruction of the faculty of spiritual discernment is His way of punishing moral depravity" (Edwards, p. 89).

In the light of this warning and exhortation, the supreme thought to be emphasized is that occupation with Christ, His Person, and Work, is the secret of progress and the safeguard against failure. This occupation with Christ will mean occupation with His Word. Originally, this was, of course, the oral word (4:13), but for us today the equivalent is the written Word. The Apostles were inspired to speak, but the only way for us to profit by their words today is through their writings, and for this reason we are told that the writings of Scripture are "God-breathed" (II Tim. 3:16). It is impossible to exaggerate the necessity and importance of the Bible in relation to the spiritual life. Just as the body requires four things for its proper condition—water, air, food, and exercise—so the Christian needs the "washing of water by the Word" (Eph. 5:26); the atmosphere of prayer; the food of the Word; and the exercise of consecration.

to any but believers; (4) The significant change of tense in verse 6, implying continuous and persistent action. A very good presentation of this interpretation will be found in an article in *The Witness* for 1922, by C. H. Hinman. It follows, therefore, that there is no reference to, still less a contradiction of, such passages as John 10:28; Rom. 8:30; Eph. 1:4, 5.

XIII

ENCOURAGEMENT

(Chap. 6:9-20)

AFTER WARNING comes encouragement. As verses 4-8 speak of the impossibility of renewal, so here we have the impossibility of failure (v. 18). Both aspects are based on divine justice. God is not unrighteous to forget what Christ has done (v. 6), and in like manner He is not unrighteous to forget what Christians have done (v. 10).

1. STRONG CONFIDENCE (vv. 9, 10)

The appeal based on the intimate word "beloved" is very striking, the expression being found only here in the Epistle. The writer is quite clearly a man such as is described in 5:2, who can "bear gently," and maintain the right balance between severity and leniency. He has a strong confidence in the people even though he had to write so severely. Perhaps the tense of the word "persuaded" suggests that formerly he had misgivings about them, but if this was so, they were at length finally settled. The emphasis on "you" is in direct contrast with the solemn teaching of the former section (vv. 4-8), the second person being used instead of the third. The basis of his confidence is the character of

God. They had been so intensely in earnest in their efforts for others, and were still maintaining this unselfish attitude that God would not forget it, and indeed we may almost say He could not, because His character is "righteous" (Prov. 19:17; Matt. 10:42; 25:40). This emphasis on God's personal character as righteous is particularly significant (I John 1:9).

2. EARNEST DESIRE (vv. 11, 12)

Then follows the expression of his eager longing that every one of them without a single exception ("each") will persist to the very end in this genuine Christian life, and especially that they will throw off the spiritual indolence or inertia (same word as in 5:11), and thereby prove that they are true followers of the faithful and patient men of old days. This appeal to get rid of their "sluggishness" may be illustrated from the report of the ill-fated Gallipoli expedition, written by Sir Ian Hamilton, in which, when describing the critical moment when an attack should have been made, said, "then came that fatal inertia." Spiritual inertia will prove similarly "fatal" in the Christian life.

This combination of "faith and patience" should be carefully noted (II Tim. 3:10). Many people are clear and even strong in regard to their "faith," and yet fail in respect of "patience." The word rendered patience in this place means literally "length of spirit," keeping things going, not easily out of breath, the opposite of shortness of temper. The word "inherit" here used in connection with the worthies of old days shows that, unlike our modern meaning of "heir apparent," they have already entered upon their inheritance. In this appeal to Christians to give diligence "unto the fulness of hope," there is good reason to render the word ful-

ness, as in the margin, by "full assurance," and there
are three elements in the Christian life recorded in the
New Testament as associated with "full assurance":
hope (as here); understanding (Col. 2:3); and faith
(Heb. 10:20). It will be seen that here again, as so
often before, emphasis is laid on continued steadfastness
in the Christian life. Conversion is not everything, because it is only the commencement, not the crown of
the believer's life.

3. HEARTY ENCOURAGEMENT (vv. 13-20)

Faith and patience are now illustrated by the life of
Abraham. God's promises were accepted by him, and
after painful endurance he obtained what God had
pledged Himself to give (vv. 13-15). But not only
did God promise, He gave Abraham an oath. These
are the two unchangeable things which guarantee strong
consolation, the promise and the oath (vv. 16-18). It is
interesting to notice the three divine oaths in this
Epistle: one referring to non-believers (3:11); one to
Christians (6:13); and one to Christ (7:21). The essential point in this divine assurance is not so much the
fact that God gave Abraham an oath, as that He did
this by associating the oath with Himself, "since he
could swear by none greater, he sware by himself"
(v. 13). This wonderful condescension shows that behind the sanctity of God's word is the sanctity of God
Himself, "an assurance made even superfluously sure."
It has been acutely pointed out that the oath came after,
not before Abraham's faith, and as a reward of his
faith concerning Isaac (Gen. 22). This revelation of
God should be dwelt on as the basis of everything.
In verse 10 He is shown to be righteous, in verse 18
He is shown to be faithful, and the purpose of this

divine assurance is that believers may have "a strong encouragement" (v. 18). They are described as having "fled for refuge to hold fast of the hope set before us, which we have as an anchor of the soul, a hope both sure and stedfast."

This thought of hope as an anchor is only found here in Scripture, but is familiar in other ancient literature, though the description of the anchor "entering within the veil" suggests a decided difference of application. An anchor in the usual sense is fixed at the bottom of the sea, and prevents a vessel from moving, but here the idea is associated with that which enables us to draw near to God.[1]

The two adjectives "sure and stedfast" suggest respectively that the ground is good and the anchor will, therefore, be enabled to hold firmly. When Christ is spoken of as a "forerunner," some think this is an allusion to the High Priest when he went into the Most Holy Place as a representative of the people, who were never allowed to enter. But Christ is more than a representative, since He does not go there instead of us, but as a pledge that we too shall go some day.

[1] The following interesting illustration is taken from Mauro's *God's Apostle and High Priest* (p. 158), but I have not had any opportunity of verifying its historical accuracy: "The figure is taken from the practice that prevailed in old times in the harbors of the Mediterranean and other inland seas. In every harbor, as may be seen indeed to this day, was a great stone (and usually there were a number of such) immovably embedded in the ground near the water's edge. That rock, as we understand, was the *anchoria* (Gr. *agkura*). It served ordinarily as a mooring for the little vessels of those days; but it also had another function. Sometimes the little ship could not, by means of its sails, make its way to a secure mooring within the harbor. In such a case, a 'forerunner' would go ashore in a small boat with a line, which would be made fast to the *anchoria*. That was 'sure and steadfast,' being of ample strength, and immovably embedded in the ground. Therefore, those on the little ship had only to 'hold fast' to the line, and by means of it, and by patient, persistent effort, gradually drew near to the shore."

Perhaps, therefore, the word is an allusion both to the High Priest and to the cities of refuge, as the phrase "fled for refuge" is found here. It seems clear, however, that the fundamental idea is not that of the sinner fleeing to Christ as a refuge, but of the believer finding refuge in the heavenly sphere, whither Christ has entered as "a Priest for ever." It has been noted that we have here three metaphors: the anchor, the refuge, and the forerunner.

As we review this solemn exhortation (5:11 to 6:20), the practical outcome is threefold. There must be the earnestness of faith, the energy of love, and the endurance of hope, for only by these can we have a continuous Christian life. There must be constant and close occupation with Christ through His Word, and then, in the power of trust and the consequent expression of loyalty, we shall be kept steadfast "even to the end."

At length, by the mention of the word "Melchizedek," the Epistle comes back to the thought with which this warning and exhortation started (5:10), and now the main theme of priesthood will receive full and proper consideration.

XIV

AN ETERNAL PRIESTHOOD

(Chap. 7:1-10)

THIS IS THE central chapter in the Epistle. At last the Priesthood of Christ is taken up with thoroughness. Was His priesthood a true one? This was the question which necessarily concerned and also perplexed the Jewish believer. It is difficult, if not impossible, for us today to understand the tenacity with which the Jews clung to their ideas of priesthood. This is shown by the way in which the Epistle deals with the subject, for only something very strong and convincing could suffice to remove and set aside the old priesthood which was at the very heart of Judaism. Christ is here shown to be a true priest, though not after the order of Aaron, but after another order, that of Melchizedek. This new idea has been prepared for, by three references to the priesthood of Melchizedek (5:6, 10; 6:20). Never before in the New Testament had Christ been called a Priest, though priestly functions as Redeemer are associated with Him in many places. To prove this priesthood it will be necessary to use the strongest possible arguments to make good the position, because Christ's priesthood, if it is to be shown to be superior to that of Aaron, must be absolute, final, and permanent. It should be carefully noted that this chapter is concerned

81

only with the *person* of the priest, not with his work, because no priestly work is associated with Melchizedek in the narrative of Genesis. For the work of the priest it will be necessary to use Aaron (8:1 to 10:18).

1. CONSIDERATION (vv. 1-3)

Melchizedek is mentioned three times in Scripture: in history (Gen. 14); in prophecy (Ps. 110); and in doctrine (as here), this last being based on the other two. The main thought seems to be just the priesthood of Melchizedek, and perhaps everything after the first three words to the last four of verse 3 should go within brackets, and not merely the section indicated in this way in our English Bible. On this view there is the one idea only: "For this Melchizedek . . . abideth a priest continually."

Melchizedek is set forth as a type of Christ in order that the Jew might see in his own Bible the proof of Christ's superiority. First, the position of Melchizedek is mentioned. He is both king and priest. No doubt, as recorded in Genesis 14, he was one of the survivors of the true religion outside the line of Abraham, for Abraham uses exactly the same title of God (Most High). This combination of king and priest is the ideal, for true priesthood should be blended with royal functions. The priest represents man to God, and the king rules over man for God. But the Epistle only deals with the priestly aspect of Melchizedek as a type of Christ, with hints here and there about the kingship. Christ is not yet literally King, nor will He be until He comes again and occupies His own Throne. The Epistle clearly indicates that at present He is not on His own Throne, but "sitteth on the right hand of the Majesty on high" (1:3; 8:1). The word Melchizedek means "King of Righteousness," and the place where he lived, Salem (afterwards Jerusalem) means "Peace." Thus we have first "righteousness," then "peace," one being the cause and the other the effect. Christ is first our righteousness, and then He thereby brings us peace (Ps. 85:10; Isa. 32:17).

The relationship of Melchizedek to Abraham is shown by the fact that the latter gave the former a tenth of the spoil, and then comes (v. 3) a very important, but somewhat difficult argument in regard to Melchizedek himself. The thought is based on the silence of the record in Genesis. The Spirit of God omitted all these details about Melchizedek in the very book which contains so many genealogies, and so the comparison is made between the silence of the record about Melchizedek and the actual facts concerning Christ. It is as though the verse said that the story in Genesis speaks of Melchizedek as without (recorded) father, without (recorded) mother, without (recorded) genealogy, without record of his birth or his death. Govett puts the matter briefly yet helpfully in these words:

"The previous history of Melchizedek is purposely closed against us by God, with the set intention that we may look at Melchizedek only as he stands *spoken of in these verses of Genesis.* He is so spoken of that he may be a perfect type of the Son of God; and hence his imperfections, which would have come out in regular biography of him, do not appear."

Taking the story of Genesis by itself, Melchizedek's priesthood is seen to be based on what he was, not on any right which he inherited. There is no record of a break in the narrative, which, so far as the actual story is concerned, suggests that he abides a priest and possesses an uninterrupted office. The element of time-

lessness in the priesthood is thus suggested. It is a
curious coincidence, and one that is helpful as an illustration that, among the bricks found at Tel el-Amarna,
which are now in the British Museum, there are some
letters written by Ebed-Tob, who was a Priest in Jerusalem after Melchizedek. He writes these significant
words: "It was not my father nor mother who installed
me in this place, but the arm of the Mighty King gave
it me." The reference to the priesthood of Melchizedek,
as without a break, is in marked contrast with the emphasis on genealogies associated with the Levitical priesthood, for their proper line of descent was carefully emphasized and scrutinized (Ezra 2:62). It is the difference between personality and legality. As we shall see
later on, the priesthood of Melchizedek is regarded as
typical of the uninterrupted tenure of Christ's Priesthood, and when it is said that Melchizedek was "made
like unto the Son of God," it shows that the Son of
God is the antitype, since it does not say that the Son
of God was made like unto Melchizedek. It is also particularly important to notice this title "Son of God,"
the divine aspect, not the human, as would be the case
if the word "Jesus" had been found.

2. COMPARISON (vv. 4-10)

Now comes a careful comparison of Melchizedek
and Abraham. The greatness of the former is seen
in the fact that even Abraham, of all men, the founder
of the Jewish nation, recognized his superiority. This
was first shown by the benefaction that Abraham gave
to Melchizedek (vv. 4-6), and by the benediction
which Melchizedek pronounced on the patriarch (v.
7). Then the argument from silence is used again,
and it is shown that in the Levitical priesthood men

who died received tithes and gifts, while in the case
of Melchizedek the record can be taken as suggesting
one who is continually alive (v. 8). Further, it is
pointed out that Levi himself could be regarded as
having paid tithes to Melchizedek in the person of his
great-grandfather Abraham. This is the argument in
which by comparison it is shown that Melchizedek is
superior to Abraham: Abraham is greater than Levi;
Melchizedek is greater than Abraham; and, therefore,
Melchizedek can be rightly considered as superior to
Levi. Thus the priesthood of Melchizedek is superior
to that of Aaron which descended from Levi. These
verses show a fourfold superiority of Melchizedek over
Abraham: (1) through human benefaction (vv. 4-6);
(2) through divine benefaction (v. 7); (3) through
human duration (v. 8); (4) through human position
(vv. 9, 10).

In this treatment of Scripture it is impressive to observe the fulness with which the Old Testament is un-
folded, indicating that it possesses a meaning far deeper
than that which appears on the surface. There are re-
ticences as well as disclosures. The fact that Melchizedek is thus conformed to our Lord is an instance of
the remarkable foresight associated with Scripture, and
is a proof of its possession of a depth of meaning which
could only come as the result of divine inspiration.

It is almost superfluous at this stage to remark again
on the necessity of the Priesthood of Christ to full
Christianity, and yet the theme already suggested needs
frequent, almost constant emphasis: "Think of Him as
Priest and I will make you understand" (Nairne).

XV

A SPIRITUAL PRIESTHOOD

(Chap. 7:11-19)

THE ADDITIONAL thought at this point is that Melchizedek's priesthood in Christ is superior to the Levitical priesthood. After the story in Genesis 14, the reference to Melchizedek in Psalm 110 clearly indicated God's intention to make a change in the priesthood.

1. THE NEED (vv. 11-14)

The purpose of priesthood is described by the word "perfection," meaning that true relation of fellowship with God which is the true end and object of man's existence. He was to be brought near, and then kept near to God, but since for the accomplishment of this the Levitical priesthood was powerless, a change was essential. With a change of priesthood there came, of necessity, a change in the law which was bound up with the priesthood, priesthood and law going together (v. 12). Priesthood was a characteristic of Judaism, and with the change of priesthood came the abrogation of the covenant with Israel, a point which is fully treated in the next chapter. The need of another priesthood is also seen from the fact that Christ as a Priest according to the order of Melchizedek did not come from the priestly tribe of Levi, but from Judah, of which tribe nothing was said about priesthood (v. 14). This reference to our Lord's descent is interesting because elsewhere it is made clear that He was of the line of David from the tribe of Judah (Acts 2:29-31; Rom. 1:3). The title "our Lord" is also important, and should be compared with "the Lord" (2:3) and "our Lord Jesus" (13:20). Thus these verses show the need of Jesus Christ as distinct from any other priest, in order that we may be brought and kept near to God.

2. THE PROOF (vv. 15-19)   QUESTION-4

The writer proceeds to give further indications of the inferiority of the Levitical priesthood. The rise of the new implies the inferiority of the old. The priesthood is not merely "another" but "different" (v. 15, Greek). Several contrasts are then instituted between the old and the new (vv. 16-18). "Law" is contrasted with "power"; the former restrains and the latter enables. "Commandment" is contrasted with "life"; the one being external, and the other internal. Flesh is contrasted with an unbreakable life; one is changing and the other unchangeable. The "foregoing commandment" is contrasted with the "better hope"; the one looks backward and the other forward. "Weakness and unprofitableness" are contrasted with that which brings us "near to God," the one being imperfect and the other perfect. Thus the old is set aside and rejected, and the new is introduced for the purpose of accomplishing the divine purpose for man.

It is important to read verses 18 and 19 in the Revised Version, when it will be seen that the setting aside or disannulling of the old commandment is put in contrast with the entrance or bringing-in of a better hope, the phrase, "for the law made nothing perfect," being put in brackets, and the word "did" of the Authorized Version being omitted. Thus, all through, the chief thought is that of drawing near to God, and the one secret of this is priesthood. Some one has said: "The people could never get along without the priesthood of Aaron, neither could we get along without the priesthood of our Lord."

XVI

A PERPETUAL PRIESTHOOD

(Chap. 7:20-25)

THIS CHAPTER, dealing with the person of the priest, shows the superiority of Christ's priesthood along four lines, of which we are now to consider the third. Because it is not subject to any change, it is a perpetual priesthood.

1. AN UNCHANGEABLE PRIESTHOOD (vv. 20-22)

This element of unchangeableness is due to the fact of a divine oath, which was not true of the Levitical priesthood. The priests of Aaron's line were inaugurated without oaths, but Christ was appointed priest by the solemnity of a divine oath (Ps. 110), and on this account He is the Mediator of a better covenant. The Greek term translated "Mediator" is etymologically connected with the idea of drawing near (v. 19), and suggests some one who stands between God and man. This reference to the covenant is the first hint of the subject of the new covenant (Jer. 31), which will be elaborated in the next chapter.

2. AN UNINTERRUPTED PRIESTHOOD (vv. 23-25)

In the Levitical priesthood there were changes due to deaths, but in marked contrast to this, Christ lives

for ever, and on this account has a priesthood which,
being uninterrupted, is unchanged and unchangeable.
It cannot be altered, and it cannot be transmitted to
any one else. The word "unchangeable" (v. 24) may
have a passive meaning, implying something unalterable,
inviolable, uninvaded, or it may have an active meaning,
undelegated, intransmissible. Both ideas are true, because Christ's priesthood is at once incapable of any
alteration or change, and also does not pass from Himself to any one else. On this account He is able to provide a complete salvation (v. 25). This verse is the
crown of the argument. Everything else in the Epistle
may be said to be included in it, for as all the truths
hitherto discussed lead up to this verse, so everything
flows from it. He is able to save completely those who
approach God through Him because He always lives
to intercede for them. But the truths here stated are
so vital and far-reaching that the verse must receive
separate and thorough attention.

Note well — The use of the word "unchangeable"
(v. 24) is another reminder of the way in which this
Epistle effectively and effectually disposes of all claims
to sacerdotalism. A priesthood that "does not pass to
another" is quite evidently unique, in the sense of being
incapable of transmission to anyone else. For this
reason, Christ's priesthood cannot be delegated to a
human being, and therefore there are not, because there
cannot be, any priests on earth. The teaching of the
two Epistles, to the Romans and Hebrews, is the best
safeguard against all forms of sacerdotalism. Romans,
in declaring justification by faith, shows how the sinner
can come to God direct without intermediary, and
Hebrews, in emphasizing the priesthood of Christ, teaches
how the believer can "draw near" continually to God,

and find in this privilege the satisfying secret of a life
of immediate and constant communion. Thus the need
of any mediation, such as is required by a human priesthood, and the consequent auricular confession, are both
obviously set aside. Some one has rightly described sacerdotalism as an attempt to sew up again the veil that has
been rent in twain.

XVII

PERFECT SALVATION

(Chap. 7:25)

THE MOST prominent place today in Jerusalem is not the spot said to represent Calvary, but the Holy Sepulcher, and this is so because of a sure insight or instinct, or perhaps a spiritual perception, that Christ is no longer dead, but alive. There is, at any rate, no doubt that the center of the Gospel in the New Testament is the living Christ. The Apostle, while truly emphasizing the death and resurrection, leads on from them to Christ's position at God's right hand and His intercession on our behalf (Rom. 8:34). In like manner, the perspective of another Apostle is not the Christ who died, but the One who lives for evermore (Rev. 1:18). This is the theme of the entire Epistle to the Hebrews, the living Christ, the heavenly Christ, and the text before us teaches truths which are really the heart and crown of the entire Epistle.

1. THE ABILITY

When it is said, "He is able to save," it should be noted that this is the third thing associated with His ability in the Epistle: He is able to sympathize (4:15); able to succor (2:18); and able to save (7:25). This ability of Christ is a truth of great importance, and one that is at the base of everything in our Christian life and experience. It is probably on this account that we find it so prominently set forth in the New Testament. "God is able to make him stand" (Rom. 14:4); "able to stablish you" (Rom. 16:25); "able to keep you from falling, and to present you faultless" (Jude 24); "able to make all grace abound toward you" (II Cor. 9:8); "able to keep" (II Tim. 1:12); "able to build you up" (Acts 20:32); "able even to subdue" (Phil. 3:21); "able to do exceeding abundantly above all that we ask or think" (Eph. 3:20). The more we are occupied with the power of the living Christ, the fuller, deeper, and richer will our spiritual life become.

2. THE ACTIVITY

When it is said "able to save," it means literally "able to keep on saving." Salvation is threefold—past, present, and future. It includes deliverance from the penalty of sin (past); from the power of sin (present); and from the presence of sin (future). Each of these is clearly taught in Scripture, and "salvation" in its fullest meaning includes them all. In this Epistle the main thought is invariably of the salvation which is at once continuous, permanent, and perfect, and in this text, in particular "keep on saving," the truth is that of the believer's continual deliverance, just as the Apostle argues that those who have been reconciled to God by the death of His Son will inevitably be "kept safe in His life" (Moule) because of our Lord's Resurrection (Rom. 5: 6-10.).

But it is not only a continuous, it is a complete salvation. He is able to save "to the uttermost." The phrase means "completely," and is only found in one other place in Scripture, where we have a very striking contrast (Luke 13:11). The poor woman was unable to lift up herself "completely," or "to the uttermost,"—that is, she was *unable* "to the uttermost," but Christ is *able* "to the uttermost." What does this mean? Surely, first of all, it means "to the uttermost" *of our need through sin,* whether this is ours through inherited disposition or through acquired characteristic. Then it means "to the uttermost" *of our circumstances,* whatever they may be, in all their difficulty, complexity, and pressure. Then it means "to the uttermost" *of our time,* covering past, present, and future. Looking back over the past, we have been saved from the condemnation and guilt of sin; looking round upon the present, we are being saved from the power, love, and defilement of sin; looking forward to the future, we shall be saved from the very presence of sin in the glorified state above. Not least of all, this phrase means "to the uttermost" *of place.* For just as our Lord sent His disciples to the "uttermost part of the earth" (Acts 1:8), so, wherever His children go today, they experience His salvation regardless of locality, since He is the same everywhere, in His saving, sanctifying, and satisfying power.

3. The Assurance

The reason why our Lord is able thus to save completely is that "He ever liveth to make intercession." God deals with the sins of the unsaved and the saved. For the unsaved He has provided Christ's work *on earth,* and people are redeemed through faith in His death. For the saved, God has provided Christ's work *in heaven,* and they are "saved by His life." In regard to the former, the unsaved, Christ is the Mediator (I Tim. 2:5), and in regard to the latter, it is important to notice His twofold work of Priesthood and Advocacy. The Priesthood, which is the theme of Hebrews, seems to refer specially, if not exclusively, to the prevention of sin, while the Advocacy, which is the theme of the First Epistle of John, seems to refer mainly, if not exclusively, to its cure. Thus, there is no need for the believer to sin (I John 2:1), and the Priesthood has been provided to prevent this (Heb. 9:24); but if he should sin (I John 2:2) there is an Advocate provided, who, while not showing any leniency ("the righteous"), will nevertheless provide an absolute sufficiency of restoration. It seems to be the thought of Hebrews, that Christ ever lives for the express purpose of guaranteeing the believer against sinning. It will be remembered that special emphasis was laid on infirmities (4:15) because our weaknesses are often the occasion of falling into sin. If, however, we use aright the glories of our Lord's Priesthood, we shall be "guarded from stumbling" and enabled to live the true life.

4. The Approach

It remains to be seen how this continuous and complete salvation may be made real to us in personal experience. There is one and only one class of people to whom this applies — He is able to save completely "them that come unto God by Him." The phrase "them that come," is literally "them that draw near" or "them that come right up." It is found seven times in Hebrews (4:16; 7:25; 10:1, 22; 11:6; 12:18, 22). It is the word for worshipers, meaning those who enter into the presence of God and realize their union and communion with Him. It includes acceptance and access, and implies assurance within and the right to the fullest possible appeal.

In view of these blessed truths, the call is clear, "Lift up your hearts." "We lift them up unto the Lord." The more we are occupied with the living Christ, and the fuller we confide in Him, the truer our consecration to Him, and the more complete our control by Him, the more thorough will be our experience, and the more effectual our witness. This verse, beyond any other, shows the essential and fundamental difference between the elementary experience of Christ as our Savior, and the deeper, richer experience of Christ as our Priest. The one atttitude looks back on the Cross with praise and thankfulness; the other looks up to the Throne with joy and confidence.

XVIII

A SUITABLE PRIESTHOOD

(Chap. 7:26-28)

Now COMES the application of all the foregoing to Christ, who is shown in every way suited to be our High Priest.

1. THE FITNESS OF CHRIST FOR US (v. 26)

After the previous discussion comes this outburst, "Such an High Priest." He is not named, but it is only too evident that the reference is to the only One who can satisfy the conditions of bringing man near to God. The phrase, "became us," is wonderfully impressive. Christ has been depicted from the standpoint of God, "it became him" (2:10), and now it is shown that "He became us." We possess because we have need. In our helplessness "He is able," and in our sinfulness "He is able to save." At this point the question may rightly be raised as to why one priest is better than a succession (7:23, 24). It has often been illustrated by the Israelite who, after enjoying the sympathy of a familiar priest of Aaron's line, found himself in relation to a new priest, and wondering whether he would be sympathetic or not. When priests were continually changing, personal characteristics did not perhaps matter much, but the Epistle to the Hebrews makes much of the personal characteristics of Christ (2:9-18; 4:14-16), and since He ever lives, His priesthood calls for careful attention.

(1) He is "holy," in the sense of reverence toward God. The word seems to indicate holiness of character, and is one of the two words in the New Testament which have been well distinguished as devout, *hosios,* and devoted, *hagios.*

(2) He is "guileless," that is, harmless, in the sense of being entirely free from all malice or baseness.

(3) He is "undefiled," that is, unsullied, free from all moral impurity or defilement.

(4) He is "separated from sinners," meaning "set apart permanently" from those sinners for whom He is said to befit us because of His unlikeness to us. While Christ has been shown to be like us (2:17; 4:14; 5:7-9), He is also unlike us; and this difference is here specially emphasized. As we have already seen, sympathy with temptation does not need experience of sin, and the very fact that He is unlike us is here, and elsewhere in the Epistle, shown to be the ground of His sympathy with us. It is scarcely possible to emphasize too often in the present day the fact that "sin was neither the source nor the result of the temptations to which He was subjected." Again and again it has been pointed out that He was not assailed by solicitations of evil, due, as in our case so often, to previous indulgence in sin, or else due to the fact of succumbing to the assaults of evil. Nor was it necessary for Him to experience every form of temptation, but only that the temptation should be thoroughly real. "Not quantitative equivalent, but qualitative resemblance" (Garvie, *Expository Times,* vol. xxvi., pp. 456, 457).

(5) He has been "made higher than the heavens." That is, He has entered into the presence of God, where no accuser can come. It would be of great value in the full understanding of this Epistle if all the texts (there are ten) found in it referring to heaven were studied together.

(6) He has no need to renew His sacrifice, which was Himself. This seems to be a suggestion of what is to follow in chapter 9, where the functions of the priesthood are treated, the work of the priest whose person is here presented.

(7) His priesthood is divinely perfect and authorized, not limited by human weakness (v. 28). Man's priesthood is associated with infirmity, but the priesthood of the Son is both perfect, in the absence of weakness, and permanent, because it is due to the divine oath which has appointed Him Priest for evermore.

Dr. Saphir calls attention to two things in this chapter: how much saving we need, and how well Christ can do it. His mediation must go low enough to reach the Cross, high enough to reach to heaven, and deep enough to enter into and abide in our hearts (Saphir, *Hebrews,* vol. i, p. 413-415). And so Christ on the Cross guarantees peace of conscience, while Christ on the Throne gives peace of heart. His death cancels our condemnation, and His life guarantees our access to the very presence of God.

XIX

THE BETTER SANCTUARY

(Chap. 8:1-6)

HITHERTO WE have been considering the Person of the Priest. Now we are to consider His Work, and see that as priest He perfectly discharges the duties of His office. Melchizedek is used to set forth the Person of the priest and Aaron to set forth His Work. This is probably due to the fact that no priestly service is associated with Melchizedek in Genesis 14, but only the *fact* of his priestly office; and so, on this account, it is necessary to turn to the priesthood of Aaron to learn what the priest has to do. Melchizedek is thus employed for the minister and Aaron for the ministry. As already hinted at, the new priest must have a new covenant (7:22), and this involves a new sanctuary (8:1-6), a new service (chap. 9), and new worshipers (chaps. 9-10). The work of the priesthood is discussed in 8: 1-10, 13. But everything of this section is really summed up in 8:1,2, where it is seen that the Priest on the throne is the minister of the true tabernacle, and He possesses a ministry as much superior (8:6) as He Himself is personally superior.

1. THE CHIEF POINT—PRIESTHOOD (vv. 1, 2)

In these verses the climax of what has already been said, and what is yet to be said, is indicated. Christ is

a Priest, a Priest on a throne (v. 1), a Priest who exercised in heaven (v. 2). Each part of this requires
close attention. "We have" indicates our present possession of this Priest. "Such an High Priest" points back
to what has been already set forth (7:26). "Sat down
on the right hand of the throne of the Majesty in the
heavens," is an indication of His royal position; and
again we see that the ideal Priest is one who is also
King, the two offices being combined in the one person
(7:1, 2). "A minister of the sanctuary, and of the true
tabernacle which the Lord pitched, not man." This is
a suggestion (which will be elaborated later) of the
earthly sanctuary being a copy of the heavenly, and
also indicating that the exercise of our Lord's priesthood
is solely in heaven.

2. THE PROOF OF PRIESTHOOD (v. 3)

The essential idea of priesthood is ministry. The
priest is a servant, and the specific form of service is
the offering of gifts and sacrifices. Christ fulfilled this
in the gift of Himself (9:13, 14). There is no doubt
that the allusion here is to the Lord's Sacrifice on Calvary, and not to anything that He now offers above.
There seems to be no question, therefore, from the
tense of the verb "offer," as well as from the general
teaching of this Epistle, especially chapter 9, that the
only offering associated with Christ is that of Calvary.
He is not (and cannot be) "offering" now, because
the fact of being seated at God's right hand shows that
He is not in the posture of an offerer, but rather in that
of one who has already accomplished His work of offering.

3. The Sphere of Priesthood (vv. 4-6)

The impossibility of Christ's earthly priesthood is
shown to be obvious from the fact that there could
not be two different lines of priesthood on earth (v. 4).
His high-priestly work may be said to have begun when
He offered up Himself, though there is a sense in which
He was not fully and completely priest until He entered
into heaven. In the Jewish type, the sacrifice and priest
were distinct, while in the spiritual reality, Christ is
both sacrifice and priest. And so this verse must be
understood as meaning, not that Christ's sacrifice on
Calvary was not essentially priestly, but that if He
were still upon earth, He would not and could not be
a priest. The Epistle is speaking of Christ as glorified
above, and the fact of His priesthood is associated with
heaven and not with the earth, the reason being that
there were priests on earth of the family of Aaron,
with which family Christ had nothing to do.

Then the character of the earthly priesthood is shown
(v. 5), and it is very significant that the tabernacle was
a copy of something that Moses was shown in the
Mount. The archetype was in heaven above, and the
structure which Moses was ordered to make was its
shadow. It is difficult for us to associate with heaven
anything so material or so constructed in different sec-
tions, but in some way God gave Moses a pattern, and
this is used to teach that our Lord's priesthood is not
connected with the earthly shadow but with the heavenly
reality, and on this account is superior to the Aaronic
priesthood, because it is exercised in heaven and not
on earth. Thus there was a contrast in the very design
of the sanctuary as well as in what went on within.
It is this that gives such special point to the truth of

the superiority of our Lord's priesthood in heaven (v. 6), for so far from any earthly priesthood being the more important, Christ's priesthood was really better because it was associated with heaven and not with earth.

It is to be noted that the thought of superiority (v. 6) is threefold: a better ministry; a better covenant; and better promises. The ministry is "more excellent" because it is heavenly not earthly, spiritual not temporal, reality not shadow. The covenant is "better" because it is absolute not conditional, spiritual not carnal, universal not local, eternal not temporal, individual not national, internal not external. The promises are "better" because they have reference to things spiritual and not to a mere earthly inheritance. In 7:22 the covenant was mentioned for the first time with Christ as its Surety. Here the covenant is connected with Him as Mediator, a wide term including the entire scope of His work. It has been said that the distinction between these two words is that the Surety pledges the fulfilment of an agreement, while the Mediator negotiates it. Christ's Mediatorship included His work as prophet, priest, and king. As Prophet, He reveals God's truth; as Priest, He provides God's redemption; as King, He bestows God's power.

From this section, we can see how completely the priest we need is provided for us in Christ. His is a present priesthood which we are to appropriate (v. 1). His work is complete, because fully accomplished (8:1; 1:3; 10:12; 12:1). It is at once royal and ministerial (vv. 1, 2), sacrificial (v. 3), heavenly (v. 5), and perfect (v. 6). Well may the Epistle burst forth once again with exultant experience, "We have such an High Priest."

XX

THE NEW COVENANT

(Chap. 8:7-13)

SINCE there is a new priesthood there must also be a new covenant, for the two go together, and the two references to the covenant (7:22; 8:6) are now elaborated by showing wherein the new is "better" than the old.

1. THE NEW COVENANT NEEDED (vv. 7, 8)

The first covenant was not perfect (Exod. 24:1-11) because it did not meet the needs of man. It was characterized by morality, but was lacking in power. And yet the real blame was not with the covenant, but with the people (v. 8)—"they" not "it." But it is particularly striking that it was God and not man who realized the inadequacy of the covenant and, in opposition to the tenacity of Israel in holding to the Mosaic covenant, it is here shown that God Himself sets it aside as inadequate.

2. THE NEW COVENANT PROMISED (vv. 8, 9)

It has been pointed out with great force that Jeremiah prophesied of this new covenant (31:31-34), when he was almost in despair in regard to the life of the nation, and when the union of Judah and Israel appeared absolutely impossible. But God knew that, owing to the unfaithfulness of the people, a new covenant was necessary, and He promised one in marked contrast with the old one in which they had not continued.

3. THE NEW COVENANT DESCRIBED (vv. 10-12)

First of all, in general, the new covenant may be considered as spiritual and inward, not fleshly and outward (v. 10). Then it is shown to be universal, not partial (v. 11), not for the priests only, but for all the people. But, proceeding to fuller detail, it is very important to observe the four blessings associated with the covenant: (1) God's law is to be put in the heart (v. 10); (2) The people are to be possessed by God as His own (v. 10); (3) They are to have a full knowledge of God (v. 11); (4) They are to have entire forgiveness of sins (v. 12). If these four realities are reversed, it will be seen that they represent in the order of experience the four chief blessings of divine grace: (1) pardon; (2) fellowship; (3) consecration; (4) obedience. Thus the covenant as expressed in these terms may be regarded as the realization of the "better promises" of verse 6. The law was to be put in the heart, not merely written on stone, thus indicating a deeper revelation. God and the people were to be united in true bonds, thus expressing a higher privilege. There was to be no need of teaching by others, thus pointing to a fuller knowledge. And sin was to be forgiven and forgotten, thus promising a greater blessing. In this statement we have one of the vital and fundamental differences between the Gospel and every form of heathenism, ancient and modern. Man has as his highest ideal, "Know thyself," but the Gospel depicts as the highest ideal, "Know GOD."

The words "I will make" (v. 8) are, literally, "I will perfect" or "accomplish," meaning that this covenant will not fail as the former one, but shall be brought to completion. The word "perfect," as elsewhere, is one of the essential key-words of the Epistle.

4. THE NEW COVENANT ASSURED (v. 13)

The treatment of this topic is brought to a conclusion by the statement that the former covenant has already been pronounced obsolete (1:11), and the fact that this announcement, through Jeremiah, was made six hundred years before the covenant was finally done away, is particularly striking. The tenses are also to be observed —"that which is antiquated and growing age-worn is near unto vanishing away."

Before leaving this subject of the covenant, one special point calls for notice. It will be observed that the covenant is said to be made "with the house of Israel and with the house of Judah," that is, with the whole Jewish nation. There is no doubt that this is the primary destination and purpose of the covenant. The promise of Israel's restoration is clear, together with the specification of benefits. Jeremiah's words are: "Lo the days are coming," and it is well known that the New Testament antitype of the Old Testament types is not the Christian Church but the Kingdom which is still future. In this Epistle the Church is only mentioned twice (2:12; 12:23). But we Christians have the spiritual reality of this covenant, which, while made with Israel, is for our benefit as well, through grace, and so we distinguish between the primary interpretation to Israel and the secondary (spiritual) application to the Church today. We now enjoy in the power of the Holy Spirit all the blessings of the new covenant, and yet there will be still further and fuller manifestations in the future for Israel, according to God's promise (Rom. 11:25-32).

One special application of this covenant which bears upon our life today can best be expressed in the words of a great teacher:

"Suppose God had swept away man for sin in righteousness, where the love? If He had only passed over the sins, without judging them, where would have been righteousness? There was infinite and unspeakable love to poor sinners, and infinite righteousness toward God" (J. N. D., *Notes on Hebrews,* p. 70).

XXI

THE OLD AND THE NEW SANCTUARY

(Chap. 9:1-10)

AT THIS POINT the discussion becomes exceptionally difficult, and great care is necessary in order that the main thoughts may be clear. It would seem as though the Apostle wishes to teach that as Jesus in His priesthood mediates a better covenant (8:7-13), so He mediates it in a better sanctuary (9:1-14). He thus shows the conditions of the new covenant, which is one of grace, not obedience. The way becomes open for him to say plainly that the Levitical system with all its glory was to be entirely superseded. The tabernacle, though beautiful and impressive, was yet incapable of bringing about that access to God which man needed beyond all else. It has been suggested that, in chap. 8:7-13, we have the two covenants; in chap. 9:1-14, the two ministries; and in chap. 9:15 to 10:18, the two covenants and the two ministries together.

1. THE CONTENTS OF THE OLD TABERNACLE SURVEYED (vv. 1-5)

At this point the entire contents of the Jewish tabernacle are given. Each item is mentioned, but it is impossible to deal with them in detail (v. 5), because the writer has one point to emphasize, the thought of the priesthood (8:1). Westcott points out that it is the tabernacle, not the Temple, that is used for spiritual teaching, because the Temple as a stationary edifice was purely secondary, and was not God's ideal for the people. The tabernacle is described as "of this world," meaning that which is local and transitory, in contrast with that which is eternal and permanent.

Each piece of furniture in the tabernacle had its own typical meaning as foreshadowing Christ. One difficulty has been raised in connection with the altar of incense, which seems to be regarded as in the Holy of Holies, but the difference of expression, "wherein" (v. 2), and "having" (v. 4), should be noted, the explanation being, pretty certainly, that "having" means *belonging to,* the connection being one of idea and use, not of place. There seems to be no doubt that the altar of incense was directly connected with the Holy of Holies in regard to spiritual meaning (I Kings 6:22). It also appears quite clear that the word should be translated "altar" (v. 4) and not "censer," because not only was the censer entirely unknown in connection with the giving of the law and the construction of the tabernacle, but with the word "altar" every article in the tabernacle here finds its mention.

2. THE USE MADE (vv. 6-10)

Then the meaning of this tabernacle is shown; and although it was a complete structure, yet its service was spiritually inadequate. It was as good as it could be, and yet the results were poor so far as man's true position to God was concerned. The entire structure suggested restriction, imperfection, limitation, and exclusion, and it was a continual parable of deeper realities (vv. 8-10). The sanctuary itself was material and local, instead of spiritual (vv. 1, 8); the sacrifices were inadequate, because they could not accomplish spiritual realities (v. 9); and the access was restricted, and could only deal with outward ceremonial purity, and not with inward holiness (v. 10). It is interesting here to observe the reference to the Holy Spirit as the Teacher of these spiritual realities. Thus, as He is the source of Scripture (3:7; 10:15), and is the Teacher of truth in word, so here He is the Teacher of truth in deed.

As we ponder all these references to the earthly tabernacle and its essential limitations, we see by contrast, as Bruce so well points out, that Christianity is a religion of access. As such, there is constant danger of hindrances being put to our freest, fullest approach to God. Gnosticism of old can be paralleled by more than one movement today. These do violence to this free, full access, which is the very life of Christianity and of our relation to God.

XXII

A BETTER MINISTRY

(Chap. 9:11-14)

Now COMES a contrast between the old and the new
ministry, and Christ's ministry is seen to be superior because it is spiritual and non-material. According to
Govett, verses 13-28 are the expansion of verses 11 and
12. The following elements of the comparison, or rather
contrast, are to be noted.

1. A BETTER PRIEST (v. 11)

According to the reading very largely adopted, the
verse refers to that which actually is, in contrast with
that which is anticipated. This implies, not that Christ
has become a High Priest of "the good things that are
certain to come," but of "the good things which have
already come." It is difficult to say which is the correct
view, especially since from different standpoints both
are true. In support of the contention that Christ is the
priest of things yet to come in the future, it is rightly
argued that the Epistle is always pointing forward. On
the other hand, Nairne and others maintain that the
change from "things already come" to "things certain
to come" is too obvious to be true, and that the whole
idea requires the thought of the good things as already
here provided in Christ. Other passages which refer to

things coming should be studied, especially because of
their outlook on to the future (2:5; 6:5; 10:1; 13:14).
But in any case the "good things" referred to have already been realized, at least in part, by means of the
Incarnation and Priesthood of Christ.

2. A Better Sanctuary (v. 11)

The "greater and more perfect tabernacle" is, of
course, a description of the presence of God, in which
our Lord as Priest ministers. This heavenly sanctuary
is another illustration of the superiority of Christ's
service (8:2, 5).

3. A Better Sacrifice (v. 12)

It was not "through the blood of goats and calves
but through His own blood" that He wrought man's
redemption (10:4). Blood in Scripture always includes
the two thoughts of a death suffered and a life offered.
The prominence given all through Scripture to the
"blood," as expressive of the atoning death of Him
who now lives for ever, is at once significant and important.

4. A Better Method (v. 12)

Christ's offering was "once for all," thereby indicating
a completed, not a repeated, work. The sacrifices of
animals had to be repeated and renewed time after
time, but the offering of Christ was made by the superior
way of something done "once for all."

5. A Better Blessing (v. 12)

It is very significant that while the Jewish priest
entered the Holy of Holies "with" blood (v. 7), Christ
is said to have entered heaven "through" (not "with")

His blood (v. 12). It was not necessary for our High
Priest to present His blood (nothing so material), but
only to present Himself (vv. 12, 24).

The description of the result of Christ's work as
"eternal redemption" is in marked contrast with the
redemption for one year, implied and involved in the
action of the High Priest on the Day of Atonement.
The phrase "having obtained" means literally "having
found for himself," and seems to be contrasted with
seeking perhaps because the High Priest sought forgiveness for himself and the people, but never really obtained it, at any rate as a permanent blessing. It has
been suggested that this phrase "having found" also
indicates effort on the part of Christ, suggesting that
His sacrificial work was not accomplished except through
difficulty. The same word is used in connection with
the believer "finding" grace (4:16).

6. A BETTER GUARANTEE (v. 13, 14)

The argument is that if the offering of animals was
capable of removing ceremonial defilements (Num.
19:9), much more will the Atonement of Christ remove
the guilt and defilement of sin. It would seem as though
two events were blended in the description of "the
blood" and were blended in the description of "the yearly
Day of Atonement," and the latter to the daily cleansing
for communion connected with the red heifer. The ashes
were apparently used to take away defilement caused
by death, and so a twofold deliverance was needed from
the guilt of sin through blood and the defilement of
death through the ashes (J. N. D., *Notes on Hebrews*,
p. 81).

By several modern writers the phrase "eternal spirit"
is thought to refer to our Lord's own spirit and not

to the Holy Spirit, implying that it was through the infinite worth of Christ's own spirit that His offering was efficacious for cleansing (Bruce, *Hebrews,* p. 338; Swete, *The Holy Spirit in the New Testament,* p. 252).

The use of "eternal" in Hebrews should be carefully noted because it is evidently one of the key-words of the Epistle, and is associated with quite a number of things (5:9; 6:2; 9:12, 14, 15; 13:20). Corresponding phrases are "evermore" (7:28); and "for ever" (5:6; 6:20; 7:17, 21, cf. v. 24; 13:8). These terms indicate the contrast between the temporary and eternal, between the momentary and perpetual, between the imperfect and the perfect.

7. A BETTER RESULT (v. 14)

The outcome of Christ's offering and ministry is now seen to be spiritual, not ceremonial. The conscience is cleansed, and not merely the flesh (v. 13). Conscience is mentioned in Hebrews five times (9:9, 14; 10:2, 22; 13:18). Then as the result follows service "to the living God," another proof of reality in contrast with what was merely symbolical. The distinction between "dead works" (6:1) and "wicked works" (Col. 1:21) seems to be that "dead works" may be in themselves associated with good things but possess no spiritual vitality, while "wicked works" are works that are essentially and absolutely wrong. The contrast is interesting to follow between these two expressions and "the good works" and "the beautiful works" mentioned elsewhere.

This section clearly teaches some of the deepest realities of the Christian life, from the commencement to its culmination, including acceptance (v. 11), access (v. 12), acceptableness (v. 14), and activity (v. 14).

XXIII

AN EFFICACIOUS MINISTRY

(Chap. 9:15-22)

THE THOUGHT of the Epistle proceeds to indicate the essential efficacy of Christ's ministry, and the covenant idea is once more taken up.

1. THE POWER OF THE NEW MINISTRY (v. 15)

Christ's full and voluntary surrender gives validity and efficacy to the new covenant. His Person gives efficacy to His work. The phrase "for this cause" seems to look back to verse 14 and on to "so that," and thus the verse supplies the link between the ministry and the covenant. It is as though it were said that because of the power of His sacrifice for eternal redemption He has been able to bring about the new covenant, which completes and renders effective the old. The death of the Messiah was a conception highly objectionable to Jews, and it was therefore particularly important to show its true meaning. As in verse 14 it is seen that the death was necessary for redemption, so now it is made clear that it is necessary for the fulfilment of the covenant which gives an eternal inheritance. The work of Christ has a retrospective effect, availing for all those who by faith accepted the promises. The inheritance contemplated by the first covenant was hindered by sins which had to be dealt with, and both here and in Rom. 3:25, R.V., the retrospective force of our Lord's sacrifice is clearly vindicated. The meaning of "the called" in this verse seems to refer to the Old Testament saints who could not inherit until sins were done away with. This is probably equivalent to "the heavenly calling" (3:1), and is a suggestion, which will be seen later on, that the Old Testament saints derived benefit from the redemption wrought by Christ (11:40).

2. THE GUARANTEE OF THE NEW MINISTRY
(vv. 16, 17)

These truths are illustrated by what happens when a covenant takes the form of a testament or will, by which an inheritance passes from one to another. This can only happen on the death of the testator. The same word in the Greek is used for "covenant" and "testament," and although the double use is difficult, there seems to be no doubt that in verse 15 the word means "covenant," in verse 16 and 17 "testament," and then in verse 18 "covenant" again. It is impossible to keep the uniform meaning of "covenant," because the death of the covenant-maker was never regarded as necessary. Christ is here thought of as priest and mediator and testator, and in each case a death was necessary. From the thought of His fulfilment of Aaron's office, we pass to the thought of His fulfilment of the office of Moses (Holmes), and it is in this that we can see the appropriateness and interest of the twofold reference to "covenant" and "testament." The rendering of verse 18 by Moffatt is a helpful suggestion, enabling us to blend the two ideas: "Hence even the first covenant of God's will was not inaugurated apart from blood." Thus the covenant of which Christ is the mediator is identified with the testament of which He is the testator. Important names can be adduced on both sides, some favoring the uniform rendering of "covenant" throughout, and others maintaining that in verses 16 and 17 only "testament" is possible. Two quotations may be added here to complete the consideration:

"Verses 16, 17: the word 'testament' is rightly used in these two verses. It facilitates the understanding of the passage to see this. Excepting these two verses, read always 'covenant'" (J. N. D., *Notes on Hebrews*, p. 83).

"The 'covenant' of which Christ is mediator is identified with the 'testament' of which Christ is the testator . . . and the covenant has, in fact, come to us in the shape of a testament which His death has made good. But the Apostle returns immediately to the former thought of covenant" (F. W. Grant, *Notes*, p. 48).

3. THE CONFIRMATION OF THE NEW FROM THE OLD (vv. 18-22)

The preceding teaching concerning death and blood is now confirmed from the old covenant by showing the place and power of blood in connection with Jewish worship. Practically everything needed cleansing by blood, and especially it is shown that without the shedding of blood forgiveness was impossible. It is important to observe once more the strong and continual emphasis on blood in the Old Testament. It is also central in the New Testament, and, accordingly, should be made central in our Christian life and testimony. Some one has well said: "The blood of animals cannot

cleanse from sin because it is non-moral. The blood
of sinning man cannot cleanse because it is immoral.
The blood of Christ itself alone can cleanse because it
is moral." Three things in Hebrews are said to be indispensable for Christian life: the blood (9:22); faith
(11:6); and holiness (12:14).

XXIV

A COMPLETE MINISTRY

(Chap. 9:23-28)

AFTER ILLUSTRATING the truth of the necessity of death for cleansing and inheritance, the Epistle returns to the thought of the efficacy of the blood of Christ, and the ministry of the new covenant is stated in its essential features.

1. THE SACRIFICIAL WORK OF CHRIST (v. 23)

The need of the cleansing is first shown in connection with the old services and then in connection with the new. "The heavenly things themselves" appear to mean the religion of the new covenant, and it is very striking and arresting to read of it in this way, and to know that it is said to require cleansing. It cannot mean "heaven," but must mean the heavenly realities connected with Christ's priesthood. Sin is thought to be everywhere, and as "heavenly things" are used by us who are sinful, we constantly need the atoning sacrifice of Christ, and never get beyond this necessity.

2. THE PRIESTLY WORK OF CHRIST (vv. 24-26)

Christ has entered God's presence on our behalf, not into any earthly human sanctuary; and His offering is

unlike that of the Jewish worship in that it needs no
repetition because it is eternally efficacious. The old
Testament sacrifices were characterized by repetition,
but the offering of Christ was made at the consumma-
tion of the ages (Gal. 4:4; Heb. 1:2) once for all, and
its efficacy abides for ever. Not only is sin "forgiven"
(*aphesis*, v. 22), but "put away" (*athetêsis*, v. 26).

3. THE KINGLY WORK OF CHRIST (vv. 27, 28)

At this point, the aspect of our Lord's fulfilment of
the type of Melchizedek as king is set forth. A comparison is first made between man's death in the usual
way and the death of Christ for salvation. Then the
second element of comparison is man's judgment and
Christ's return. The thought is, that as death is a
definite end of man, with nothing afterwards but judgment, so Christ's death was final, and there is nothing
further to be done in regard to sin. As man, after
death, will be brought into judgment, and cannot return
to make a fresh start on earth, so Christ died once,
and cannot come back to try again, for if His earthly
work were a failure, it is something which cannot be
set right. But it is not a failure, as His coming again
will prove, for He is to appear, quite apart from sin
and a sin-offering, with a view to everlasting salvation,
and on this account we are to look eagerly for Him.
There is, of course, no warrant for distinguishing between those who look and those who do not look. The
idea of a partial rapture is not deducible from this text,
or indeed from any other in the New Testament. In the
first place, salvation all along, from regeneration to
resurrection and rapture, is by grace and not by works,
and further, it is often forgotten that the vast majority
of the millions of Christians who have already passed

away through the centuries could not be described as among "them that wait for Him," and yet we are sure that, as part of the Body of Christ, they will be taken up to be for ever with the Lord.

It has been often pointed out that this chapter is the best illustration and explanation we possess of the meaning of Leviticus 16, just as it may be said that the best explanation of this chapter is found in Leviticus 16. Four parts of the High Priest's work on the Day of Atonement are used here to express spiritual realities in Christ. The High Priest superintended the offering of the sacrifice outside the tabernacle. Then he entered into the Holy of Holies with the sacrificial blood. Thereupon he presented the blood by sprinkling it on and around the Mercy Seat. And afterwards he returned out of the tabernacle, having accomplished his work. These four actions can be well described as indicating and symbolizing our Lord's Atonement, Access, Appeal, and Advent. The truths are helpfully summarized in verses 26-28, where we find three of the four aspects. In verse 26, His appearance in the past for Atonement; in verse 24, His appearance in the present as our Priest; and in verse 28, the promise of His reappearance at His Advent.

XXV

THE BETTER SACRIFICE

(Chap. 10:1-10)

HERE COMES the beginning of the end of the argument. For the purpose of making everything thoroughly clear, the truths already stated are recapitulated, but with significant and very important additions. As hitherto seen, the repetition of the Jewish sacrifices shows their inefficacy, and the sacrifice of Christ is seen to be superior because, He having fulfilled God's will, meets the need for a sacrifice which should take away sin. In His priesthood Jesus Christ mediates a new covenant in virtue of a better sacrifice.

1. THE INEFFECTIVENESS OF THE OLD SACRIFICES (vv. 1-4)

The "for" of verse 1 links this subject with the verse immediately preceding, and at the same time may perhaps be regarded as resuming the entire subject. It suggests that the imperfection should have led them to Christ.

(1) The old sacrifices were the shadow, not the substance (v. 1). The word "shadow" means outline, and "image," the true representation as a picture. Some writers distinguish between the "shadow" as indicating

122

the Old Testament religion, the "image" as representing the New Testament religion, and "the things" pointing forward to the reality hereafter in heaven. But it is perhaps better to understand the phrase "image of the things," as expressing present reality, though, of course, with its fulness hereafter.

(2) The old sacrifices involved repetition, not remission (v. 2). If the sinner had offered a sufficient atonement, there would have been no need of more, and therefore there would have been no fear or doubt. As it was, the constant repetition involved constant questioning. "He who is obliged to take a medicine every hour to keep life in him cannot be said to be cured" (Govett).

(3) The old sacrifices maintained a consciousness of sins, not a cleansing (v. 2), or it may mean "conscience" in the sense of recognition of guilt. This recollection of sin means a realization of what was really unforgiven, while forgiveness is intended to be connected with obliteration from memory (9:9; 10:11-14).

(4) The old sacrifices meant remembrance, not removal of sin (vv. 3-4). The essence of the question is here stated. The sacrifices were by nature inadequate because the animals were at once involuntary, not voluntary; and material, not spiritual. The result was that it was "impossible that the blood of bulls and goats should take away sins." The word "remembrance" means "an awakening of mind rather than an external making of remembrance" (Nairne). It is the same word that is used by our Lord in instituting the Last Supper, "in remembrance of Me," and the contrast is very striking. When we "remember" Him, we are recalling One who has blotted out our sins and remembers them no more (8:12).

2. The Efficacy of Christ's Sacrifice
(vv. 5-10)

Now, in marked contrast, it is shown how and why
the sacrifice of our Lord was able to accomplish that
which was impossible by animal sacrifices.

(1) The source of the sacrifice is the will of God
(vv. 5-7). The essence of Christ's offering of Himself
was His willingness to do what God required. "Lo, I
come to do thy will, O God." There is a difficulty in
connection with this quotation from Ps. 40:5-8. The
Hebrew reads: "Mine ears hast thou opened" (lit.
"digged"), while the Greek text from which the quotation is made reads: "A body hast thou prepared me."
On the principle that the Greek reading is the harder,
it may be regarded as the original, and this is the view
taken by some writers. By others it is suggested that,
whilst the Hebrew speaks of obedience, the Greek makes
special reference to the organ of obedience. This would
make the Greek an interpretative gloss, an enlargement
to meet the sense by indicating, not one faculty only,
but all, and thereby suggesting obedience. It has been
well pointed out that this Greek version was a translation made by the Jews themselves, and was not Christian, so that there can be no charge of correcting, still
less of falsifying the text. The fundamental thought,
in any case, is that sacrifice itself was a figure, and that
obedience constituted the true sacrifice. This is the last
of three important Old Testament references in this
Epistle: Psalm 110; Jeremiah 31; Psalm 40.

(2) The character of the sacrifice is obedience to the
will of God (vv. 8, 9). Herein is stated the moral
quality of the sacrifice in contrast with the Levitical
offerings. Instead of animal sacrifices we now have the

willing surrender of Christ to the will of God, and the former offerings are therefore done away in order that the latter may be established as the one and only way of forgiveness and approach to God.

(3) The purpose of the sacrifice is sanctification in the will of God. Sanctification here means consecration, not purification (13:12). It is a ritual, not a moral term, and refers to the removal of all hindrances to fellowship, and not to the inward renovation of the soul. It must never be forgotten that not once in this Epistle is sanctification associated with the Holy Spirit. Indeed it can be said that sanctification in Hebrews is almost equivalent to justification in Romans, both referring to our position, not to our condition. But there is this vital difference of standpoint: that justification deals with position in relation to God as Judge, while sanctification deals with position in relation to our fellowship with God and our approach to Him in fellowship. Christ's offering as a perfect expression of divine righteousness possesses consecrating virtue; and, through this offering, believers are consecrated in and by the will of God.

XXVI

THE CROWNING PROOFS

(Chap. 10:11-18)

THE ARGUMENT is concluded by two more proofs being adduced of the completeness and efficacy of the sacrifice of Christ:

1. FIRST PROOF: CHRIST'S PRESENT EXALTATION (vv. 11-14)

(1) The priest of the old covenant is first described (v. 11). He stood in the tabernacle, in the attitude of service. Not only was there no seat in the tabernacle, but his standing was a reminder that sin was ever present, and needed to be put away. His work involved a daily ministry, and he was always offering the same sacrifices which could not accomplish what was required in the taking away of sins. Thus man's deepest need was always kept in view, and the way was prepared for something which would prove effectual and efficacious.

(2) The priest of the new covenant is then described, in marked contrast with the old (v. 12-14). Instead of many sacrifices, Christ offered ONE. Instead of the offerings being made "oftentimes," Christ offered "one sacrifice for ever." Instead of the attitude of standing, Christ, having accomplished His work, "sat down on

the right hand of God." It is a question whether the
words "forever" should go with the preceding "sins"
or the following "sat down." Are we to understand
"one sacrifice for sins for ever" or "for ever sat down"?
Authorities are to be found on both sides, and one
suggests that we are to understand both (Holmes). But
the thought is not so much "for ever" as "continuously"
(Greek). This attitude of sitting implies authority. This
means that there is no need for Him to rise because His
work is done. The word is found four times in this
Epistle, and is only said of Christ (1:3; 8:1; 10:12;
12:2).

But there was one element lacking in the completeness of the entire work. "From henceforth expecting
till his enemies be made his footstool" (v. 13). He has
done His part, but there remains the solemn and sad
fact that every one will not accept what He has accomplished, but many will persist in hostility. In regard to this, there is nothing to do but to wait the
time appointed, "when his enemies are made his footstool." This is the feature in Psalm 110, which, up to
the present, had not been emphasized. Then the statement is closed by indicating the wonderful completeness
of His sacrifice. "By one offering he hath perfected for
ever them that are sanctified" (v. 14). This means that,
by the one offering of Himself, He has completed the
blessing for those He is setting free from sin. In verse
10 the offering is said to be the means of our consecration, while here those who are being consecrated are
regarded as realizing the end and object of their being,
in the moral and spiritual perfection—that is, the ripeness and maturity—of experience, which is the culminating point of the believer's life.

2. Second Proof: The Perfect Fulfilment
of all Conditions (vv. 15-18)

Now come the last words, clinching the argument.

(1) *The Witness of the Holy Spirit.*— Here, again, with great significance, the Holy Spirit is mentioned. Not only is He the author and source of the divine message in Ps. 3:7, and of the true meaning of the tabernacle (9:8), but He is shown to be witnessing through the statements of Scripture to the reality and power of the new covenant. This is the true witness of the Spirit, not something dependent upon our own variable emotions, but that which is objective to us, and fixed, the Word of God.

(2) *The Work of the Spirit* (vv. 16, 17).— The passage of Scripture already used in connection with the covenant (8:10-12) is here summarized, and associated with the Holy Spirit. The law is put into the heart, and into the mind; and then the love of God is shed abroad in the soul by making real His blessed forgiveness (Rom. 5:5).

(3) The great conclusion naturally follows (v. 18). *God's Will, written on the heart by the Holy Spirit,* is the proof of the sufficiency of Christ's sacrifice, and there is no need of repetition or supersession. "By promising to forget, He has forgiven, and therefore no more sacrifice in plea of forgiveness is necessary" (Wickham).

And now the writer's case is proved. All that the law meant and foreshadowed has been fulfilled in Christ. We have the threefold revelation of God in this passage, a very definite spiritual and practical exemplification of the Holy Trinity, in the *will* of God (v. 9), the *work* of Christ (v. 12), and the *witness* of the Spirit (v. 15). The old covenant meant bondage: the new, liberty; the old spoke of fear, the new of assurance; the old emphasized distance, the new, nearness; the old spoke of separation, the new speaks of fellowship.

XXVII

APPROPRIATION

(Chap. 10:19-25)

THE ARGUMENT is now closed. Jesus Christ, the Son of God, is the perfect and perpetual Priest. Because He is Son, He is priest; and because He is priest, He is a perfect Savior (chap. 5:9; 7:25). Now comes the application (10:19 to 13:25); we are to experience and enjoy all these great realities. Spiritual wealth, like every other form of riches, does not consist merely in possession but in knowledge and use. Grace needs appropriation if it is to be operative. We see here, as before (4:14-16), the association of "having" and "let us"; because we possess, we ought to use and enjoy.

1. PRIVILEGES POSSESSED (vv. 19-21)

(1) *Present Approach.* — "Having, therefore, brethren." The term "brothers" is another indication of the affectionate relations between the writer and his readers. It is found here and in three other places (3:1, 12; 13:22). Special notice should be taken of the word "having," which, as elsewhere, always implies a present and conscious experience. It is impossible to exaggerate the "present tenses of the blessed life," of which this is one. We are so apt to associate the Christian life either with the past (had), or the future (shall have),

that we often lose blessing and power through the forgetfulness of our present possibilities.

(2) *Perpetual Access* (vv. 19, 20).—Once again we are reminded of the need of boldness (3:6), indicating inward confidence and outward courage. This boldness is intended to be exercised in relation to the "holiest," that is, the presence of God. Unlike the high priest who alone could enter the Holy of Holies, once a year only, all believers now can enter into the presence of God at all times. This is due to the fact that we approach God by virtue of the sacrificial atonement of Jesus, which is described as "a new and living way," which He has inaugurated, or consecrated, or dedicated (9:18) for us. The reference to the way as "new and living" is unusually interesting, because it tells of the perpetual freshness of the offering of Christ. The word translated "new" means freshly slaughtered, and suggests that the sacrifice of Christ never grows old. As Luther says: "It seems but yesterday that Jesus died on the cross." We are accustomed to express this when we sing:

> Dear dying Lamb, Thy precious blood
> Shall never lose its power,
> Till all the ransomed Church of God
> Be saved, to sin no more.

No wonder the Apostle speaks of the "precious blood of Christ" (I Pet. 1:18, 19). There is one difficulty in the text which needs attention. When it is said "through the veil" most commentators regard the following words, "that is to say, His flesh," as explanatory, but elsewhere the veil is regarded as that which keeps man from God, hiding Him instead of revealing Him, while Christ's human nature is never set forth as that which separates man from God. One writer endeavors to interpret it by saying that the veil of the tabernacle, whilst a real barrier, was only thin and could be lifted up. In the same way, Christ's physical nature made Him near to man, and it was rent by death, and thus became a passage to God. But it seems in every way more natural, from the standpoint of spiritual interpretation, to associate the word "flesh" with "way," thereby showing that it was our Lord's human nature, the Incarnation, which was the way to God. It is true that this is not so natural (though quite possible and legitimate) in the light of the Greek text, but it is decidedly more in keeping with the New Testament general view of our Lord's earthly life, and of Himself as the way to God (John 14:6).

(3) *Perfect Assurance* (v. 22).—We possess a High Priest over the house of God, and on this account there is perfect and perpetual approach, with no hindrance and every help.

Thus these verses sum up the blessings of the new covenant, involving real access to God founded on a real atonement which enables us to approach. Hitherto the imperfections of the old covenant have been seen in three directions: the sanctuary, the ministry, and the offering. Now these threads are gathered up, and it is shown that Christ is in the heavenly sanctuary, and is engaged in a spiritual ministry based upon His offering on the cross. The House of God is the community of believers (3:6), and after the truths emphasized in chapters 8 and 9 it is possible to see the appropriateness of the reference to the "blood of Jesus" and to the entrance into the Holiest. Christ is not only our representative, but we are regarded as identified with Him. In chapter 9 it was shown that He had entered God's presence, and now (10:19) we can enter.

2. PRIVILEGES USED (vv. 22-25)

Three times the words "let us" are found, and in each case one of the Christian graces is specially mentioned.

(1) *The Exercise of Faith.*—This is the upward attitude. We are to "draw near," continually making use of the entrance which is ours, not standing aloof, as was the case under the old covenant (Num. 18:22). We are to do this with a genuine heart, in thorough sincerity, and in full confidence based on trust. This is possible because our hearts, that is, our entire personalities, are "sprinkled from an evil conscience," and, like the priests who were consecrated, "our bodies are washed with pure water" (cf. Exod. 29:4). Thus our faith can rightly be exercised, because of the fulness of provision in Christ for us.

(2) *The Exercise of Hope* (v. 23). — This is the forward attitude. The original text, as the Revised Version shows, refers to "hope," and not to faith. It is difficult to know why the Authorized Version used the word "faith" over again. We are to continue to "hold fast" the confession of our hope (3:1; 4:14) "without bending"—that is, with firmness in the face of anything that would tend to deflect us from our position. The reason for this is the faithfulness of God (11:11). This emphasis on the divine character is the foundation of everything in our life; because He is faithful, we are to have faith and hope (I Cor. 1:9; 10:13; I Thess. 5:24). Once again it is noteworthy that the Epistle is ever pointing forward. This reference to hope emphasizes the spirit of expectation, which should always characterize believers.

(3) *The Exercise of Love* (vv. 24, 25).—This is the

outward attitude. We are to "consider" one another, with the special object of stirring our fellow-Christians to love and "beautiful works." Already we have been exhorted to "consider him" (3:1), and now we are to "consider one another," while Paul adds that we are to "consider ourselves" (Gal. 6:1). The use of the word "provoke" is a beautiful paradox. It expresses the Greek word, which is transliterated in English by "paroxysm." This is the only "exasperation" which is permissible, and it is impossible to have too much of it. We are to "exasperate" our fellow-Christians in the sense of "provoking" or inciting them to "love and good works."

But there was one particular way in which they could do this, "by not forsaking the assembling of ourselves together, as the manner of some is; but exhorting one another." Already there were Christians who were withdrawing themselves from their fellow-believers, and isolation is a certain danger and involves inevitable weakness. While we are justified in relation to Christ solitarily and alone, we are sanctified in connection with other Christians, and we shall never know what it is to be a "saint" unless we make much of "the communion of saints." Dr. Mackintosh has well pointed out that the word saint never occurs in the singular, and that "invariably it is plural" (*The Divine Initiative*, p. 100). There was a very definite reason for maintaining this fellowship, "so much the more, as ye see the day approaching." They were apparently on the eve of the great catastrophe of A.D. 70, the destruction of Jerusalem, and for Christian gatherings to be left and slightingly considered under such circumstances was to incur the greatest possible spiritual peril. Then, as at all other times, "Union is strength."

XXVIII

"DO NOT DESPISE"

(Chap. 10:26-39)

Now comes the fourth of the interposed messages of warning. The thought seems to be closely connected with the preceding verse, suggesting that if we forsake our fellow-Christians, it may easily lead to our forsaking Christ. It will be seen that the substance of this message is still more solemn than those which have preceded it. The dangers of apostasy are forcibly indicated, and the underlying appeal is that they should not despise the message of the Gospel.

1. WARNINGS (vv. 26-31)

(1) *The Possibility* (v. 26).— After receiving the full knowledge of the truth, it is only too possible to continue to sin willingly (3:12; 6:7). The reference to the "full knowledge" of the truth seems clearly to indicate a spiritual experience, and not intellectual information alone. The tenses are also expressive because they point to persistent sin. The evil seems to be somewhat like the presumptuous sin of Num. 15:30 and Ps. 19:13. It evidently means a sin that deliberately goes against God and right.

(2) *The Prospect* (vv. 26, 27).—Negatively such an attitude shows that there is no more sacrifice for sin,

for there is nothing in reserve because it would be like "crucifying the Son of God afresh" (6:6). On the contrary, there is a solemn prospect of judgment which is certain to have a punitive and even destructive effect (Isa. 26:11).

(3) *The Principle* (vv. 28, 29).— Under the old covenant the man who despised the law died without mercy after the evidence of two or three people. But under the new covenant the sin is still greater, and the judgment will be greater as well. The references to the "blood" and "the Spirit" shows the senses of solemnity with which realities of the new covenant are to be met (9:15-18). The phrase "spirit of grace" is unique in the New Testament, and is doubtless taken from Zech. 12:10. Reference has already been made to the "throne of grace" (4:16). Nothing could be more terrible than the description of the one who deliberately spurns and despises the most sacred and precious realities of the Gospel of Christ. He is described as one who has "trodden under foot the Son of God," "counted the blood of the covenant an unholy thing," and "hath done despite unto the spirit of grace." It is obvious that this is no case of ordinary backsliding, but, as in chapter 6, of wilful and persistent apostasy.

(4) *The Proof* (vv. 30, 31).—The Old Testament revelation of God is clear (v. 30), though the different usage of the passages quoted should be noted (Deut. 32:35, 36, or Ps. 135:14; cf. Rom. 12:19). In the Old Testament the reference is to the divine vindication of Israel in the face of enemies, but in the New Testament the reference is to the divine vengeance on His people in vindication of His character. Then the passage goes on to state the essential character of God as "living"

(3:12; 9:14). It must never be forgotten that the Gospel, with all its freedom and grace, does not modify in the slightest degree the character of God as holy, just, and true. In these respects the revelation of the new covenant is identical with that of the old. While we have "entrance," it is into the "holiest" (v. 19).

Before passing on to the next section the connection between the three warnings of chapters 2, 6, and 10 should be observed. From indifference (chap. 2), it is not difficult to proceed to rejection (chap. 6), and from this it is a short step to contempt (chap. 10). It is a reminder which we do well to heed, that "grace is not operative whether we believe or not."

2. REMINDERS (vv. 32-34)

Just as in chapter 6, the warning is followed by a message of encouragement. Their past is to fortify them for the present.

(1) *Past Privilege* (v. 32).— They are called upon to "keep on reminding themselves" (Greek) of old days when they were spiritually illuminated. This effort to recall the past is a proof of the reality of the dawn of spiritual life in their soul. But the change here is the reverse of that seen in 6:8, 9. There the third person is followed by the second, while here the second is followed by the third. But the essential idea is the same. The case described in verse 20 is apparently one of pure hypothesis in contemplation of a possibility which did not apply to them.

(2) *Past Power* (vv. 32-34).— They had endured amidst a conflict and a persecution. This was in part their own personal experiences of being made "a gazing-stock by reproaches and afflictions," and partly it was a matter of Christian fellowship, since "they became

companions of them that were so used." This endurance was exemplified in a twofold way, by sympathy with prisoners, especially with the writer of the Epistle, and by the actual loss of their own possessions. But the explanation of this endurance was clear. They knew that they had themselves, as united with Christ, "a better and an enduring substance." Some read a slightly different text, "knowing that ye yourselves have in heaven a better and enduring substance." It is impossible to avoid comparing this passage with our Lord's words about acquiring our own souls by patient endurance (Luke 21:19).

3. COUNSELS (vv. 35-39)

(1) *The Exhortation* (v. 35).— The warning fitly closes with earnest advice. They were not to cast away their courage and boldness (3:6). This means, as it has been pointed out, not that they were to come back to where they had been, but that they were not to go back from where they then were. The reason for this exhortation is that there was awaiting them "great recompense of reward," another allusion to the fact that this idea of reward is an integral part of the Christian revelation concerning the believer's life (11:26).

(2) *The Need* (v. 36).—Meanwhile the one necessity was endurance, a patient, deliberate continuance in faithful loyalty to Christ. Once more the thought of the blend of "faith and patience" is emphasized (6:12). The reason for this patience is that "after ye have done the will of God ye might receive the promise," another hint of future blessing, their outlook being always fixed on that which was to come (11:39).

(3) *The Support* (vv. 37-38).—The outlook was inspiring because it would only be a little while until their

Master would come without fail (v. 7). In the meantime they were to look up in faith and live the life of trust in a present Savior and Lord. If by any possibility they were to draw back, God would cease to find satisfaction in them.

(4) *The Challenge* (v. 39).—The "we" is emphatic, as much as to say that this reference to drawing back has nothing to do with us. The meaning of "draw back" is, literally, to "take in sail" (Gal. 2:12). The believer is depicted as a sailor who, instead of opening every stitch of canvas he possesses to catch every breeze, deliberately strikes sail and thus becomes becalmed. Drawing back in the Christian life is sometimes due to disappointment, at other times to depression, at still others to discouragement, but always to distrust. This negative assertion is appropriately followed by the declaration that not only are we not going to shrink, but we are "of them that believe to the saving of the soul." The word "saving" does not refer to what we generally understand as salvation from sin, but is a word meaning "complete possession." Faith is first receptive in spreading its sails to catch the breeze of God's revelation, and then it is responsive to His Word and grace. The believer may be said to "possess" his soul partly in this life, and fully hereafter. Thus the message is twofold—we are to "draw near" and "draw not back."

XXIX

THE MEANING OF FAITH

(Chap. 11:1-3)

IT IS IMPORTANT to see this chapter in relation to the preceding context. In chapter 10:22-25 there were three exhortations, respectively to Faith, Hope, and Love. These are elaborated in turn: chapter 11 dealing with Faith; chapter 12 with Hope; chapter 13 with Love. But this chapter is also closely connected with the thought of faith in 10:38, 39, with its reference to endurance based on the promise, which has Hab. 2:4 as its key. The danger of these Christians was living by sight, not by faith. It is interesting to observe the three occasions on which this passage from the Old Testament prophet is found in the New Testament. Each seems to have a different emphasis. In Rom. 1:18 the emphasis is on righteousness—"the *righteous* by faith shall live." In Gal. 3:11 the emphasis is on faith—"the righteous by *faith* shall live." But here the emphasis is on life—"the righteous by faith shall *live*," because this chapter deals with the faith that enables a man to live, not merely to enter into the blessings of salvation, but to retain them from the beginning to the close of his earthly life.

1. The Description (v. 1)

It is important to notice that this verse is not a definition of faith in itself, but only a description of its effects. The word "is" is emphatic. Faith is described in a two-fold way. It is the foundation of things hoped for, and the "conviction (or proof) of things not seen." The word rendered "substance" or "foundation" indicates that faith must have a basis—the Word of God. And so the vital question is not "Do we believe?" but "Whom do we believe?" It is not a case of sincerity of belief, but of the truth of what is believed. This verse has been variously rendered. By one writer thus: "Faith is the very substance of the things we hoped for; the irrefutable proof of the invisible transactions." Another renders it: "Faith means we are confident of what we hope for, convinced of what we do not see." This indicates that faith gives substance or reality to our hopes and puts to the test the things we do not see. It is very interesting that in certain papyri unearthed in Egypt the Greek word translated "substance" or "assurance," R.V., is found in the technical sense of "title deed," the root idea being that they "stand under" the claim to the property to support its validity. It is certainly a very suggestive rendering to translate this verse, "Faith is the title deed of things hoped for." It will be seen throughout the chapter that faith is not passive but active certitude, and it would appear as though all the illustrations are either concerned with "things hoped for" or "things not seen."

2. The Testimony (v. 2)

After describing faith we are told that it was in reference to faith that the elders of the former dispensation, some of whom are going to be mentioned in detail, received from God a testimony to their life of faith. These "elders" are called a "cloud of witnesses" (12:1).

3. THE PERCEPTION (v. 3)

With great appropriateness the story of faith commences with creation and might almost seem to be illustrated by Adam, although he is not mentioned. The word rendered "worlds" is "ages," and refers not so much to the material creation as to the world regarded from the standpoint of time. There are four senses of "world" referred to in the Bible, and unfortunately they are not properly distinguished by different English words. There is (1) the earth as material, the word *ge;* (2) the world as an ordered creation, *kosmos;* (3) the globe as inhabited, *oikoumene;* and (4) an age, *aion.* The last mentioned is the name used here, and it seems to refer to what may be called time-worlds, the idea being that the various ages or dispensations were planned by God with reference to a goal, toward which all are moving. Perhaps, therefore, the verse suggests both Creation and Providence, especially as the word "framed" means adjusted. This verse is thought to give the secret of the faith of the elders (v. 2) who did not judge by appearances but understood that the dispensations were prepared by God, and consequently they believed He would overrule everything for the accomplishment of His purposes.

XXX

THE MANIFESTATIONS OF FAITH

(Chap. 11:4-16)

HERE COMMENCES the list of examples of faith, with special reference to the Patriarchs.

1. FAITH'S WORSHIP (v. 4)

Abel's offering is described as "more excellent" than that of Cain, and it is natural to ask wherein lay the superiority. Many people think it was quite natural for Cain to bring the produce of the ground in accord with his own position as a tiller of the ground, just as it was natural for Abel, a shepherd, to bring a lamb. But Abel's offering is said to be "by faith," and this was the secret of its greater excellence, for faith is always a response to a divine revelation. God must, therefore, have spoken about sacrifice and the way of approach to Himself, and many think that there is an allusion to this in God making coats of skins for Adam and Eve (Gen. 3:21). But whether this is so or not, it is clear that the "more excellent" sacrifice was due to its being offered in God's way, not man's. There does not seem to be any doubt that this thought of faith responding to the divine revelation about sacrifice is the obvious belief of the writer of the Epistle. The result of this faith on the part of Abel is that God testified to his righteousness (v. 7; Rom. 10:10), and as a result Abel is still speaking by telling of the necessity of blood-shedding for acceptance with God (9:22).

2. FAITH'S WITNESS (vv. 5, 6)

Enoch is the next illustration of the faith by which we live, and his translation is said to have been due to his life of faith. God testified to His pleasure in His servant and then "took him" (Gen. 5:22). The chapter pauses at this point to show the absolute necessity of faith if we are to be well pleasing to God. We must both believe that God exists and that He is accessible to those who earnestly seek Him. Once again the characteristic word "cometh" is used. It is found seven times in Hebrews descriptive of worshipers. Here also is the second of three indispensable things emphasized in the Epistle: the blood (9:22); faith (11:6); and holiness (12:14).

3. FAITH'S WORK (v. 7)

Noah is used as an illustration of another aspect of faith, that which has to do with ordinary everyday life and service. The divine oracle warned him beforehand of what was coming, and he proceeded with reverence to prepare the ark, whereby he accomplished a twofold work—that of saving his own house and of condemning the world around him. Year after year he was building the ark and preaching righteousness (II Pet. 2:5), because, unlike those around him, he believed what God had told him. The result was that he became an inheritor of true righteousness.

FAITH'S WALK (v. 8)

Abraham illustrates the obedience of faith. On being called he promptly and fully obeyed with unquestioning trust. He did not know whither he was going though, as the Greek implies, he was "certain to receive" the place for an inheritance. God had told him this, and as the divine word was so real he did not hesitate to surrender certainties at home for what seemed to be uncertainties, except for the fact that God's Word was the most assured reality in his life.

5. FAITH'S WAITING (vv. 9, 10)

It is harder to wait than to work, but Abraham's passive life was as full of faith as his active. It was a severe test after having received the assurance of the gift of the land. Yet he dwelt in temporary habitations, followed by his son and grandson, who, like him, had the same promise. The explanation was that Abraham was expecting something far beyond the earthly Canaan. While he knew that that would be given yet there was something infinitely more, "the city" which was solid and real because God was its "builder and maker." This is a striking testimony to the reality and reach of Abraham's faith.

6. FAITH'S WILLINGNESS (vv. 11, 12)

Sarah was also an illustration of faith, and is probably mentioned because, as Westcott points out, she was so closely united with Abraham that her faith was due to his influence. The explanation of her faith is God's faithfulness. This is always the case, our trust answers to His truth; our faith to His faithfulness; because faith is the human response to the divine revelation. The outcome of this faith on the part of Abraham and Sarah was a seed at once heavenly and earthly. The "stars of the sky" may suggest the heavenly seed, the Church of God, the Body of Christ. The "sand" may

illustrate the earthly seed, the Jewish nation, the kingdom of Israel.

7. FAITH'S WELCOME (vv. 13-16)

These verses sum up the present section, and point
out that all the Patriarchs died full of faith, though
they never actually received the promises, but having
seen them "afar off" were persuaded that God would
be true to His Word, and they welcomed the blessed
assurance of certitude by, as it were, "embracing" the
divine word of promise, meanwhile confessing that they
themselves were "strangers and pilgrims" because their
hopes were fixed on something infinitely greater than
an earthly inheritance (v. 14). In all this there was
no compulsion, because if they had desired to return
to their earthly life they could have done so without
any trouble or difficulty. But they were so certain of
God and of the spiritual realities promised by God
that their desires were directed towards "a better
country," a heavenly, and on this account we have the
remarkable assertion that "God is not ashamed to be
called their God." Nothing could be more inspiring
than this thought that God is not ashamed of His
people (2:11). We are often tempted to be ashamed
of Him, but in proportion as we are loyal and true
to God, there is a sense in which we may say with
reverence that He is proud of us and takes pleasure in
the fact that we are showing forth His praises to those
who are indifferent to Him.

XXXI

THE DETERMINATION OF FAITH

(Chap. 11:17-28)

WE ARE NOW to consider various aspects of faith as illustrated in the lives of some of the outstanding men in the early history of Israel. The main thought seems to be that of faith exercised in the face of improbabilities (vv. 17-22) and perils (vv. 23-28).

1. ABRAHAM (vv. 17-19)

It was a real test of Abraham's faith that he was called to offer up Isaac (Gen. 22:1), especially because after having waited twenty-five years for the coming of his son, Isaac was the one in whom was centered all his hopes based upon God's promise. That this severe trial should come to him after all that had happened was, indeed, a test of his faith, but he rose superior to any thought of unbelief, and showed to the young men with him that he fully expected to bring his son back with him (Gen. 22:5). His faith somehow or other grasped the wonderful possibility of the power of God raising Isaac from the dead at once. Abraham does not seem to have had any doubt about being required to put his son to death, but he felt sure that God "was able to raise him up," and metaphorically

147

this is exactly what happened (v. 19). It is all the more impressive to note this conviction about the resurrection, because up to that time no instance of resurrection had been known, but like Sarah, who judged God to be "faithful who had promised" (v. 11), Abraham was assured that "God was able." As it has been well asked: "Do we ever lose anything by trusting God in the dark?" (J. G. B., *Notes*, p. 62). Test was thus met by trust.

2. ISAAC (v. 20)

The blessing of Isaac on Jacob and Esau had reference to the realization of the divine promises, and it is particularly striking that this blessing was bestowed at the end of the patriarch's life, so that just as his days on earth were closing his mind was occupied with "things to come."

3. JACOB (v. 21)

In the same way Jacob, when he was almost at the point of death, blessed his two grandsons, and acknowledged the presence of God by his attitude of worship. After much wandering in life he showed his conviction of the reality of the future in this blessing and worship.

4. JOSEPH (v. 22)

It is also interesting to observe that Joseph is here mentioned in connection with the end of his life. Notwithstanding all that surrounded him in Egypt he had respect to the future in the fulfilment of God's promises about the return to Canaan.

In these three instances the men were at the close of their days, and yet their hearts were full of expectation, their faith was indeed the "substance of things hoped for."

5. MOSES (vv. 25-28)

It is noteworthy that Moses occupies more attention than any other in this list of men and women of faith, and the prominence given to him is full of striking suggestion in regard to his faith in God.

(1) *Courageous Love* (v. 23).— God was honored in the simple faith of the parents of Moses. We do not know why the babe's beauty should have been specially mentioned here, but in any case "they were not afraid of the king's commandment," and with simple yet strong confidence in God they hid their little one.

(2) *Definite Refusal* (v. 24).— Notwithstanding all the magnificent opportunity that lay before Moses in his adoption by the daughter of the king, he deliberately refused to be regarded as her son, basing his refusal on an estimate of the comparative value of the glory of Egypt and the position of God's people. We note the significance of the statement, "when he was come to years of discretion," implying that the decision was made when he was in the full vigor of manhood.

(3) *Deliberate Preference* (v. 25).— With combined insight and courage he chooses, and casts in his lot with the people of God, even though it meant the endurance of affliction. The enjoyment of the "pleasures of sin" must have been a real attraction to a man of his type, and yet, rather than experience these, he deliberately sided with God's people. The pleasures of sin are only "for a season," but the people of God have "pleasures for evermore" (Ps. 16:11). There is no doubt as to

the actual fact of "the pleasures of sin," but behind
these will always be found, however hidden away, the
"deceitfulness of sin" (3:13).

(4) *Careful Consideration* (v. 26).— In the face of
great advantages Moses weighed the possibilities at-
tached to Israel and to Egypt. In the former case he
knew there would be "reproach," and in the latter
"treasures." But he looked beyond the wealth of Egypt,
and felt that even though he had to suffer hardship
"the reproach of the Messiah" would be "greater riches
than the treasures in Egypt."

(5) *Clear Prospect* (v. 26).— The reason of this
definite choice was that "he had respect unto the
recompense of the reward." Once again the thought of
reward is seen to be associated with the believer's life
(10:35), and it is important to remember that there
is a reward of grace according to works. We are saved
by faith in the completed work of Christ, but our faithfulness as followers of Christ will be rewarded hereafter in proportion to what we have done. "Behold, I
come quickly, and my reward is with me" (Rev. 22:12).

(6) *Whole-hearted Action* (v. 27).— When the time
came, Moses was ready to forsake Egypt, not feeling
in the least afraid of the anger of Pharaoh. He endured everything because he saw and knew Someone
who was infinitely greater and more powerful than even
the great king of Egypt. It is striking to read that "he
endured as seeing him who is invisible."

(7) *Simple Obedience* (v. 28).— He was so conscious of the presence of God that it was perfectly
natural for him to obey God's Word and keep the
Passover.

The faith of Moses calls for special attention from
all who would live the life of trust. We see three

things: (*a*) Faith's vision. Moses saw through temporal things and penetrated to eternal realities because he saw God (v. 27). (*b*) Faith's value. Moses chose, reckoned, separated himself, and determined to do the will of God. (*c*) Faith's victory. He overcame the world as represented by Egypt, the opposition of Pharaoh, and the power of his own natural tendencies as he was tempted by the glories of Egypt.

XXXII

THE DIFFICULTIES OF FAITH

(Chap. 11:29-38)

ANOTHER SET of illustrations of faith in the remarkable variety of its power and influence is now to come before us.

1. FAITH AND THE WORD OF GOD (vv. 29-31)

(1) *At the Red Sea* (v. 29).— The contrast here is between faith and unbelief, the Israelites crossing the Red Sea because of their confidence in God.

(2) *At Jericho* (v. 30).— The contrast here seems to be between man's weakness and God's power. Nothing could have been more absurd from the military standpoint than the action of Israel in connection with Jericho, and yet, notwithstanding any conflict between human ideas and God's directions, the people obeyed God and the result was seen.

(3) *Rahab* (v. 31).— A modern author has written helpfully on "Religion in Unlikely Places," and this is certainly true of Rahab, for it would have seemed incredible that she exercised faith unless we were told of the fact, but her confession of trust in the God of Israel shows that, with all her former wickedness, there was a genuine belief in the one true God.

2. FAITH AND ACTIVITY (vv. 32-34)

After these detailed references comes a series of names and actions, illustrating the exploits of faith. Seven names are first given (v. 32), and then a number of varied and various examples are afforded of what faith was able to do in life.

3. FAITH AND PASSIVITY (vv. 35-38)

Now the thought turns to what faith can endure, the emphasis being on the sufferings of the people. Faith enables as well as equips, and through faith people can suffer and be strong.

The chapter closes (vv. 39, 40) with a summary statement about all these worthies whose faith was acknowledged by God, though they did not obtain what God had promised. The reason for this was that God's time had not come. He did not intend them to be placed by themselves. They had to wait for us, and now, through Christ, the Old Testament saints have been put in a better position, and are able to share in the spiritual blessings provided by Christ. The entire Epistle is occupied with this thought of the inferiority of spiritual privileges under the old covenant compared with those which are our portion now. Thus, in the old days, sin was set aside, while now it is sent away; in the old days, sins were constantly remembered, now they are completely removed. Christ, as depicted in the completeness and glory of His work (see chaps. 1-10), has actually provided the "better things," which God all along had foreseen for them and for us. When it is said that "they without us should not be made perfect" we have again the thought of "perfection," so characteristic of this Epistle, referring to the mature

and ripe experience which was only possible when
Christ the Son of God and our High Priest accomplished
His work on our behalf.

The whole chapter is so full of vital teaching on
faith that it seems important to review it in the light
of the need and place of faith in the Christian life.

(1) *The Value of Faith.*— We can see in the chapter
what God thinks of it. Through faith He is able to
declare a man righteous (v. 4) and well pleasing (v. 5).
Because of His people's faith He is "not ashamed to
be called their God" (v. 16). The world is "not
worthy" of such people (v. 38), and God bears witness
to the fact of faith in His followers (vv. 2, 39).

(2) *The Power of Faith.*— What it does for man is
evident all through the chapter in a variety of ways.
It has been said that just as there are three verbs—
to be, to do, and to suffer—so the Christian is called
upon to be, to work, and to endure, and faith is the
power whereby we are enabled to fulfil all God's will
for us.

(3) *The Secret of Faith.*— The chapter tells us how
faith accomplishes results. It is due solely to the fact
that God is the object of faith. Faith is convinced that
God exists (v. 6), is capable of bestowing blessing
(v. 6), is faithful (v. 11), is able (v. 19), and is ever
present with His people (v. 27). Some one has said
that the believer, like David of old, has five pebbles
available for use: God is, God has, God does, God can,
God will. All these are clearly and abundantly illustrated in this wonderful chapter.

XXXIII

THE RACE

(Chap. 12:1, 2)

THE CONSIDERATION of the worthies mentioned in the former chapter leads to exhortation to patient endurance, especially in the light of the greatest witness of all, Jesus Christ (v. 2). The characteristic thought of the entire chapter is Hope. The assurance of the future prospect is intended to lead to endurance in the present.

1. THE PROSPECT

The Christian life is illustrated as a race, "the race that is set before us." The Greek word is the usual one for "contest." It is interesting to note that in the Book of Acts, Christianity is several times spoken of as "the way" (19:9, 23).

2. THE PREPARATION

For the purpose of running this race, the Epistle exhorts believers to "lay aside every weight and the sin which doth so easily beset." This distinction between "weights" and "sin" is important. A weight is something superfluous, an encumbrance, something that is not necessarily evil. Moffat renders the word by "handicap," which, however, another scholar sets aside. There are many things in the Christian life that may be called "weights," involving choice rather than obliga-

155

tion. Some one is recorded to have asked whether a certain thing would do a person harm, and the reply was given, "No harm, if you do not wish to win." There are many things in life which have to be set aside if we would realize to the full the will of God for us. Like an athlete in running a race, it is essential to "lay aside" everything that might hinder. When mention is made of "sin" the question at once arises whether any particular form of evil is intended. It is at least suggestive that the phrase is *"the* sin" (Greek), the article being used, and some have thought that it refers to the specific sin of unbelief in contrast with the remarkable examples of faith found in the former chapters. The phrase "easily beset" is literally, "well surrounded," the idea apparently being that of a robe in a race, which because it would cling closely around the form has to be laid aside.

3. THE EFFORT

"Let us run with patience." This combination of special effort with determined endurance is very striking. It is a reminder of the three aspects of life set forth by the prophet (Isa. 40:31), mounting up, running, and walking. It is not difficult to put forth special exertion; the real test of life is the steady, normal progress of the soul — "not paroxysms of effort but steady endurance."

4. THE INCENTIVE

"Compassed about with so great a cloud of witnesses." There is no doubt that the reference is to the worthies in chapter 11, whose life was such a fine testimony to their faith. The word here is "witnesses," in the sense of those who testify. Westcott points out that the word does not and cannot mean spectators. It would have been quite easy for the Greek word meaning "eye-witness" to be used, but it is significant that it is not found. It has been tempting to many writers to speak of our race being run in an arena surrounded by spectators, as though those who have passed on before are still interested in our welfare. But, however attractive the idea, it is impossible to derive it from this passage.

5. THE INSPIRATION (v. 2)

Each part of this verse calls for special attention. "Looking" means either "looking off" from those mentioned in chapter 11, or looking away from every distraction. The word "Jesus" is also striking because, as elsewhere, this word when used alone in the Epistles always refers to the human person, our Lord in His earthly life. He is described here as "the author and finisher of faith." The word "our" must be omitted, as the reference is to Christ's own faith. The word "leader" is found in 2:10, and also in Acts 3:15; 5:31. It means the one who stands at the head of the long procession of those that believe. The word "finisher" means the one who has manifested faith in its complete form (10:14; 11:40). Christ showed in His life the perfect realization of faith. Then He is described as having set before Him the joy of complete redemption, and on this account "endured the cross, despising the shame." The suffering was the proof of His faith, and because of this patient endurance He has become permanently "set down at the right hand of the throne of God." "He who trod the path before us, and trod it perfectly to the end" (quoted by Nairne).

It is interesting and valuable to bring together the various names given to Christ in this Epistle: Son, Apostle, High Priest, Leader, Perfecter.

XXXIV

THE CONTEST

(Chap. 12:3, 4)

THE THOUGHT of spiritual athletics is here continued
with special reference to our Lord's endurance. Believers are further incited to continue, notwithstanding
all the hardships. "Who dares turn back in the face
of this magnificent throng?"

1. THE GREAT STRUGGLE

"Such contradiction of sinners against Himself." Our
Lord is here shown to have been continually facing
hostility from sinful men, and the story of the Gospels
reveals this only too plainly.

2. THE GREAT DANGER

"Lest ye be wearied and faint in your mind." This
was the peril against which he would warn them. Christ
endured and did not faint (Isa. 40:28), and they are
solemnly urged not to lose heart.

3. THE GREAT COMPARISON

"Consider him." The word means to compare, to
weigh in the balance. It is only found here in the
New Testament, and is literally identical with our word
"analogy." It seems to suggest that the experience of

the suffering believers to whom the Epistle was written was "analogous" to our Lord's experiences.

4. THE GREAT LIMITATION (v. 4)

"Ye have not yet resisted unto blood, striving against sin." By some this is interpreted to mean that they had not yet been tested to the point of martyrdom, though on the other hand it is thought that the Epistle was written too early for any wholesale persecution involving martyrdom. On this account it is suggested that the reference is to the fact that they had not been in deadly earnest, the next verse suggesting something like blame. According to this view their sin would be a failure to persist, and it is thought that this is the best meaning of the phrase "striving against sin" in the light of the context. The Old Testament ideas, of which this Epistle is full, associate blood and life, and it is therefore implied that the striving here had not reached the heart of things, their life-blood. This would mean an exhortation against that half-heartedness which is so outstanding a feature of the warnings in this Epistle. Their life would thus be properly described as "anemic," not sacrificing. Yet another suggestion is that of their relation to others, that in their strife against wrong-doing in others, they had not at that time gone to the length of complete resistance.

Thus the Christians are exhorted to endurance in the face of the great example of Christ.

XXXV

THE TRAINING

(Chap. 12:5-11)

AT THIS POINT there seems to arise the question why it was not possible to have fellowship with Christ without all this endurance. The answer here given is that the fact of suffering, however mysterious, is inevitably associated with the education of faith.

1. THE DIVINE MEANING OF DISCIPLINE
(vv. 5-10)

The terms used here show that the example of Christ is no longer in evidence as in the earlier verses, because He was never chastened. The words used are all expressive of discipline and chastisement, not judgment and punishment. It is shown that the training is not even the education by a schoolmaster, but the action of a father who desires his children to be children in reality. The discipline is, indeed, a proof of sonship (Prov. 2:11, 12), and it is "for discipline that you have to endure." This is the true purpose, and fatherhood does not involve weakness.

2. THE TENDERNESS OF THE DIVINE PURPOSE
(v. 10)

The contrast between the human and the Divine Father is here stated, in the contrast between pleasure and profit, God's sole intention being that we may be partakers of His very character of holiness.

3. THE PRESENT EXPERIENCE (v. 11)

Discipline invariably appears at the time to be a matter of pain, and not of gratification. Our minds usually fail to realize anything more than the suffering of the present.

4. THE FUTURE OUTCOME

But notwithstanding our short memories, God's discipline is invariably for our good, in order that there may be fruit in our lives as shown by a genuine righteousness of conduct.

5. THE PERSONAL ATTITUDE

This is suggested by the phrase, "they which are exercised," and everything depends on the attitude which we take towards suffering. We are not to forget, not to despise, not to faint (v. 5), but we are to endure (v. 7), and to be in subjection (v. 9). When this attitude is realized, then we understand the direct and blessed connection between "discipleship" and "discipline."

XXXVI

THE DUTY

(Chap. 12:12-17)

AT THIS POINT several exhortations are given with special reference to the discipline already mentioned.

1. OUR DUTY TO OURSELVES (vv. 12-15)

"We are to 'lift up' the hands which hang down, and the feeble knees." This appeal to avoid relaxed arms and weakened knees is directed against the despondency which was only too apt to overtake these suffering believers. They were also to make straight paths for their feet (v. 13). This means that their conduct was to be straightforward. Depression is only too apt to make us careless and indifferent to the life we live. They were to be vigilant, being concerned both with the state of their heart within and the character of their life outside.

2. OUR DUTY TO OTHERS (v. 13-15)

There was a danger lest this disregard of true life should lead others astray. "Lest that which is lame be turned out of the way." The influence of the Christians on those around is direct, profound, and continuous. They were also to "follow peace with all men." The word "follow" is literally "pursue," like the hunter and his game, or the athlete and his race. And their vigilance was specially intended to prevent "any root of bitterness springing up" which might cause trouble to themselves and also to others.

3. OUR DUTY TO GOD (vv. 14-17)

They were not only to "pursue peace," but also "holiness," without which no man shall see the Lord. This is the third indispensable thing mentioned in the Epistle (9:22; 11:6). The thought of "pursuit" is very striking, and is often found in the Bible, both in the Hebrew and Greek (Ps. 23:6; 34:14; Rom. 12:13; 14:19; Phil. 3:12, 14; I Thess. 5:15; I Tim. 6:11). Notice the threefold very impressive "lest" (vv. 15, 16). The first means failure to go forward. They were not to come short of God's purpose (4:1). The reference is clearly to the loss of spiritual privilege, not to their eternal salvation. The second indicates bitterness as opposed to harmony (Deut. 28:19). The third shows the results that would accrue if these exhortations were not heeded. The first sin mentioned is that of impurity. The second is associated with Esau who is called a "profane person," but the word "profane" has its old meaning of "secular," not its modern specific idea of the use of blasphemous speech. There are few words that are more suggestive by way of illustration than this. It comes from the Latin words *pro-fanum*. Outside every fane or temple there was an area of land open to every one, where people gathered, an open place without enclosure. In contrast with this was the sacred enclosure of the temple or "fane" itself. Esau had no such sacred enclosure in his life, and in this sense was a purely secular man. In the one act of selling his birthright for a "morsel of meat," he revealed his essential character as one who did not possess God in his life (*Notes,* by F. W. Grant, p. 70 f.). A careful consideration of the original shows that the verse does not mean that Esau, in spite of his repentance, was rejected by God, but that "he found no way of changing his father's mind," though he sought *the blessing* with tears. Spiritual things were insignificant with him up to this time, and when he realized what he had done, it was too late to obtain what he had spurned.

XXXVII

THE INSPIRATION

(Chap. 12:18-24)

NOW COMES a description of the goal Faith and Hope. It seems intended to enforce the last paragraph, especially the words of verse 17, though it also summarizes the whole. The antithesis of the old and new covenants is in line with the contrasts found all through the Epistle. Now comes the final and culminating illustration, "not Sinai but Sion." Instead of occupying their minds with their present sufferings, they were to lift up their hearts and contemplate what God had provided for them.

1. THE OLD COVENANT (vv. 18-21)

The main thought is that Mount Sinai was marked by terrors and concerned with things material, and in particular involved a distance from God. There are seven points mentioned in these experiences as included in the circumstances of the giving of the old covenant. (Read Exodus, chapters 19 and 20). The reference to the words of Moses (v. 21) is not in the Old Testament account in Exodus, but is similar to what is found in the Septuagint of Deut. 9:19, and is in accord with Jewish tradition.

2. The New Covenant (vv. 22-24)

In contrast with Sinai comes this reference to Mount Sion; instead of terrors are glories; instead of the material, the spiritual; instead of distance, access. Here, again, there is a sevenfold description. There seems to be a distinction (v. 23) between the early Christian Church, the believers of the first day, "the Church of the first-born," and the Jewish believers of the Old Testament, "the spirits of just men made perfect." This distinction is also seen in 11:39, 40. Again the word "Jesus" is used expressive of the human nature and earthly life of our Lord, and is particularly appropriate to the context. It is also very striking to read "ye are come," especially when it is remembered that up to the present there have been only exhortations: "Let us come boldly" (4:16); "let us draw near" (10:19-22). Thus, those who are appealed to in this way are regarded as having already the spiritual position in Christ which they are to make their own. The word "better" is found here for the last time, twelve occurrences altogether being found in the Epistle. By contrast with verse 18, "ye are not come," it is seen that the key-thought is that of access, "ye have come right up" (v. 22).

XXXVIII

"DO NOT DEPART"

(Chap. 12:25-29)

THIS IS THE fifth interjected warning and fitly closes the series (2:1-4), against drifting; 3:7-14, against disbelieving; 5:11 to 6:20, against degenerating; 10:26-39, against despising. The immediate context seems to suggest the occasion for it. The "blood that speaketh" (v. 24) is now shown to be equivalent to "Him that speaketh" (v. 25), and after the glowing description of the new Society (vv. 22-24) the readers are urged to abide therein and to show themselves worthy of it.

1. THE WARNING (vv. 25-27)

(1) *The Possibility* (v. 25).— A comparison is again instituted (as in 2:2, 3) between the old and new dispensations, showing the greater responsibility of being associated with the latter. Responsibility is not only not lessened; it is really increased by the Gospel. Grace though free and full is nevertheless inextricably bound up with seriousness and faithfulness of life. The word "refuse" is the same as "entreated" in verse 19 and as "excused" in Luke 14:18. "See that you do not beg off from Him who is continually speaking." And it

167

is to be observed that if we begin by "excusing," we may easily end by definite "turning away." We commence by "deprecating," and we finish by "departing."

(2) *The Peril* (v. 26).— A contrast is instituted between "then" and "now," and between "earth" and "heaven." Thus, the greater importance of the Gospel appeal is again clearly indicated and emphasized. (See Exod. 19:8; Hag. 2:6, 21.) The phrase "once more" seems to suggest a final appeal (only once more) and the divine voice should be considered in the light of the statement (in 1:1, 2) that God has spoken supremely and finally in His Son.

(3) *The Purpose* (v. 27).— The reason of this divine movement is to sift and test, so that the transient elements may disappear and the permanent ones remain (II Pet. 3:10). This passage is often employed to show that the present age, like the first century, is a time when beliefs and institutions are being shaken in order to make more evident the things that cannot be changed or even "shaken." The entire Epistle has been thought to indicate the unshakeable realities that abide essentially the same under all circumstances. Careful students of Hebrews can discover for themselves what these are; and compare what they find with the following:

(1) The Fact of God's Being and Character (chap. 1). This means that, notwithstanding every human vicissitude, His Presence and Authority are always the same.

(2) The Revelation of God in the Person of Christ. The Incarnation of a Divine Christ (chap. 1) and the appearance of a true Man (chap. 2) are abiding facts (13:8). God has approached man.

(3) The Reality of Christ's Personal Experiences during His earthly life (chaps. 2-5). Whatever happens, nothing can affect the fact of the life of the man Christ Jesus as recorded in the Gospels.

(4) The Redemptive Elements in Christ's work (chaps. 5-7). The "Jesus of history" was not merely or chiefly a Teacher, but primarily a Savior, and this fact abides in spite of and after the severest criticism of the New Testament teaching.

(5) The Provision of Spiritual Blessing in Christ (chaps. 7-10). By His Death, Resurrection, and Ascension, Christ is shown to be the Fount of grace for human life in the present, and notwithstanding everything that opposes or disappoints, this grace is "sufficient" for every need (II Cor. 12:9; 9:8).

(6) The Possibility in human life of "all things that pertain to life and godliness" (II Pet. 1:3) being realized and enjoyed through faith (chap. 11). Nothing has yet shaken in the slightest degree the testimony that "by faith" all that man needs can be and is received and utilized.

(7) The Certainty of the ultimate triumph of Christianity in the revelation of the Lord from Heaven to usher in and establish His Kingdom (chap. 12). Amid all earth's upheavals this "blessed hope" is one of the strongest pledges of complete victory.

These or their equivalents seems to be the great realities which the Epistle records as unshakeable, and they are all summed up in the great statement that Jesus Christ is unchangeably the same (13:8), a fact that He has proved and pledged by His resurrection (13:20).

2. THE EXHORTATION (vv. 28, 29)

Based on the warning comes a fitting exhortation.
They are "not to cling to what God is shaking to
pieces, or they too will suffer shipwreck."

(1)) *Our Continual Privilege.*— We are constantly
and perpetually (Greek) receiving a Kingdom that is
incapable of being shaken. Christianity is stable, and
this is our unspeakable satisfaction.

(2) *Our Continual Need.*—"Let us have grace." The
words may mean "let us hold fast grace," or, as Westcott and other writers suggest, "let us show gratitude."
(See also margin of American version, here, and I Cor.
10:30.) Either would be suitable, while, of course,
both are true. We need continual grace for daily lives,
and our bounden duty is constant thanks.

(3) *Our Continual Call.*—"Serve God acceptably with
reverence and godly fear." The thought in the Greek
is that of priestly service, and is to be rendered with
awe and reverence. We are all priests unto God (Rev.
1:6), and our attitude to Him must always be characterized by reverence. "Holy and reverend is his name."
The freeness of grace is perfectly compatible with the
fulness of awe. God is not only our Father; He is our
God (I Pet. 1:17). In these days, when so often "evil
is wrought by want of *thought* as well as want of *heart*,"
we do well to remember how much and how often
the Bible speaks of "the fear of God."

(4) *Our Continual Reminder* (v. 29).—This is the
stern side of the Gospel. The words refer to believers,
for they speak of "our God," and show His true character. It is a reminder of the words of the prophet
who asks, "Who among us can dwell with the de-

vouring fire?" and then answers by showing that it can be accomplished by the man who speaks and does what is right (Isa. 33:14-16). Thus, fire is (as elsewhere) both a symbol of divine judgment and also (as here) of the divine character of holiness.

And so the exhortation to Hope closes with a solemn appeal to live in the present as befits those who possess such a kingdom and who anticipate such a future.

XXXIX

IN INDIVIDUAL LIFE

(Chap. 13:1-6)

THE APPEAL for love (10:24) is here taken up, as faith and hope have already been in preceding chapters. Love is exemplified in various ways, and first of all in connection with the personal life of each believer.

1. IN RELATION TO ALL CHRISTIANS (v. 1)

The phrase "brotherly love" is not quite adequate because the termination "ly" means "like," and the reference is not to "brotherly love," but to actual "brother-love." We are not to love as though we were brethren, but because we are brethren. This is a Christian grace, and it is probable that our Lord had this in mind when He spoke of the "new commandment" (John 13:34, 35). Three times in two verses, and thus with a significant emphasis, we read the words "one another," and the newness of the love seems clearly to refer to the object, for nothing else about love could be called "new commandment." There had been the love of parents and children, the love of patriotism, the love of pity and philanthropy, for ages before this time, and the highest standard of love had long ago been taught in the familiar words, "Thou shalt love the Lord thy God with all thy heart, and with all thy soul, and with all thy mind, and with all thy strength" (Deut. 6:4; Mark 12:30). This feature of love to our fellow-Christians, simply because they are Christians, is a prominent feature of New Testament religion, and it almost seems as though the very word for this brother-love, which is so familiar to us as "philadelphia," was coined as the result of this Christian attitude (I Pet. 1:22; 2:17; II Pet. 1:7). This "brother-love" was one of the finest testimonies to the reality of the Christian profession, and we know how Tertullian was able to refer to it as an evidence among the heathen: "See how these Christians love one another." This brother-love was one of the ways in which the Christians would keep together in the face of much that was trying and troublesome (10:25).

2. IN RELATION TO NEEDY CHRISTIANS (v. 2)

This may almost be called "stranger-love." Hospitality is another feature of primitive Christianity, which we do well to ponder. It is clear from the New Testament that it was realized as a duty incumbent on Christians, and in those days, when brethren traveled from place to place, it is easy to see its necessity and value as one of the marks of true Christlike fellowship (Rom. 12:13; I Tim. 5:10; Tit. 1:8; Heb. 13:2; I Pet. 4:9). The allusion to the story of Abraham and the angels is clear (Gen. 19).

3. IN RELATION TO SUFFERING CHRISTIANS (v. 3)

The believers are urged to remember those that were in bonds as though "bound with them," and they are to keep in mind those who were suffering adversity because they themselves were still in the body and so liable to the same afflictions. This seems a more natural meaning than that which is offered by some, that "the body" means the Church, and that the thought is of oneness in the body of Christ (I Cor. 12:27).

4. IN RELATION TO PURITY (v. 4)

This counsel is intended to apply to all, and was specially directed against laxity on the one hand and asceticism on the other (I Tim. 4:3). All who transgressed this law would be dealt with by God.

5. IN RELATION TO CONTENTMENT (vv. 5, 6)

The word "conversation" means "life," not speech, and refers to conduct, which was to be "without covetousness and marked by contentment." The basis of this contentment is the Word of God responded to by faith. It is very striking to see the contrast between what "He hath said," and what as a consequence "we may boldly say." The former reference is not found in so many words in the Old Testament, but it is an obvious adaptation of several passages (Gen. 28:15; Deut. 31:6; Josh. 1:5; Isa. 41:17). The latter quotation is taken from Ps. 118:6.

In all these counsels the ruling thought is that of love because, when that actuates the soul, there will be the greatest possible care both in regard to our practical duties to others, our relation to the persons of others, and above all our attitude to God in regard to His provision for our lives. Love will express itself to brethren, to strangers, to the suffering; love will respect the rights of others, and will be content with what we possess, because we are able to say with confidence that "the Lord is my helper."

XL

IN SOCIAL LIFE

(Chap. 13:7-14)

FROM THE PERSONAL naturally comes the corporate aspect of the believer's life in which also love is to be shown.

1. IN THE LIGHT OF PAST MEMORIES (v. 7)

They are urged to be true to the teaching of former leaders, and they are to imitate their faith, bearing in mind the issue of their conduct.

2. IN THE LIGHT OF PRESENT REALITIES (v. 8)

Amidst everything else that was changeable, Jesus Christ remains ever the same. It is very striking to notice this verse flanked on both sides by verses containing ideas in marked contrast. Like a great mountain in the midst of the sea, Jesus Christ stands ever the same. In view of the fact that we are now over eighteen centuries from the time that Jesus Christ was on earth, it is a marvelous claim to make on His behalf that He is always the same. Of no one less than God could this be said. Here is the rock foundation for our life, "Jesus Christ, the same yesterday, and today, and for ever."

3. In the Light of Present Dangers (v. 9)

They are urged not to be carried about like driftwood on the wave by various and strange teachings. The heart should be established by grace, not by food. Holiness does not depend upon food, but upon grace; and the Christian is "not under law, but under grace" (Rom. 6:14).

4. In the Light of Present Privileges (vv. 10-12)

This is intended as an illustration of the grace already mentioned, and it is important to keep the context strictly and constantly in mind if the text is to be properly understood. There is no emphasis on the word "we" in "we have," which is simply equivalent to "there is," and is exactly like the similar phrase in verse 14. Thus all idea of an antithesis between Jews and Christians is at once set aside, for this thought would rob the context of its harmony. In view of the fact that the Epistle is written to Hebrew Christians, there is no doubt that the phrase "We have an altar" means that there is in the Jewish religion an altar, at which eating could not take place. And this is further explained by the "for" of verse 11, where it is pointed out that the bodies of the animals were consumed, not eaten. Then verse 12 with its "wherefore" is the lessor to be drawn from this statement. Jesus Christ is the antitype of the sin-offering, to which the allusion is evident. It is as though the writer said: "There is (among us Jews) a sin-offering, the flesh of which they who serve the tabernacle (*i.e.*, the priests) have no right to eat." The rules for the sin-offering are clearly stated in Lev. 4, and arguing from these the writer means: "The Jews have one particular kind of sacrifice whose flesh the priests have no right to eat. It is the sin-offering. The bodies of those victims are burnt, not eaten. Wherefore, Jesus, the true sin-offering, that He might sanctify the people through His own blood, suffered without the gate of the temple and of Jerusalem, His death answering to the death and burning by fire of the type outside the tabernacle and camp." The idea of eating from an altar is only found here, and must, of course, mean partaking of a sacrifice. But nothing was ever eaten which was once put on the altar, for everything laid thereon was only taken off in the form of ashes.

It is important to keep this interpretation clearly in view, because there are those who associate the passage with the Lord's Supper, to which it cannot possibly refer, because the entire context refers to something which is *not* connected with *eating,* while the Lord's Supper is obviously an ordinance at which eating takes place. So far from the reference being to the Holy Communion, the writer seems to be combating the very error implied in the view that the Lord's Supper is a propitiatory sacrifice. Then, too, the word "altar" was never used of anything material, like the Lord's Table, until the time of Cyprian in the third century (see Westcott, *Hebrews*). "Altar" and "table" are contradictory terms, and eating from an altar would be impossible and repulsive to a Jew. The term "altar" is, of course, used for "sacrifice."[1]

---

[1] Nairne (Cambridge Greek Testament, *Hebrews,* p. 129) has a very suggestive paraphrase of these verses under the heading which he calls "The Sacrament of Calvary": "It is a noble thing to have the heart founded deeper by simple grace. But rules of food are mean—a trivial disappointing round. We are beyond such cares; the ministers of the tabernacle partake of the sacrificial food; our altar is of a different

5. In the Light of Present Duties
(vv. 13, 14)

This is a call to separation, based on the fact that our Lord suffered outside the city of the Jewish people. As Weymouth well puts it, we are to go forth "sharing the insults intended for Him." It is very striking that the believer is shown to occupy two positions in this Epistle. In 10:9-16 he is regarded as inside the veil with his conscience purged, with a spiritual position that is permanent, and with an access to God which is constant and perpetual. But here he is regarded as outside the camp, living a life of separation involving experiences of suffering, and yet one that is marked by perfect satisfaction because he is in fellowship with his Lord, who has similarly suffered. This call to separation is specially pointed by the thought that in the present life we do not possess a continuing city, but like the pilgrims of old (11:10, 16) we seek the city that is to come.

Here, again, it is easy to see the principle of love in these various and social relationships. It is love that enables us to recall the past, and thank God for those who have taught us the Word of God. It is love which enables us to rejoice in the consciousness of Christ's enlarging and enjoyable grace. It is love that enables us to avoid present dangers, and to rejoice in present privileges, even though they are accompanied by present suffering. The Christian knows that suffering is to be followed by glory in the city of God on high.

order. Indeed it is in outward appearance more analogous to the place outside the camp where the refuse of the high priest's sacrifice was (as we read) burnt. It was on Calvary, outside Jerusalem, that Jesus, in order to sanctify the people of God, suffered as a criminal."

XLI

CLOSING WORDS

(Chap. 13:15-25)

A FEW CLOSING thoughts are now given, though up to the very end the main truths of the Epistle are kept clearly in view.

1. THE PRACTICAL PROOFS (vv. 15-19)

A fourfold call is made, and at each point the life of the believer is required to show the reality of his profession.

(1) *A Call to Praise* (v. 15).—This is one of the three sacrifices of the New Testament which the believer in Christ can offer (v. 16; Rom. 12:1). These have been aptly described as the Christian's person, purse (American *pocket-book*), and praise, or to put it otherwise: himself, his substance, and his songs. But why should praise be called sacrifice? A sacrifice is something that *costs,* and it would seem as though praise could not be described in this way. Perhaps, however, it refers to the testimony of those early Christians when their witness to Christ by word was indeed "costly," sometimes to the extent of persecution and death. But even for us it is essential to keep in mind that true praise will always be far more than the expression of

words. It will involve a genuineness of utterance, "The fruit of our lips giving thanks to his name" (Hos. 14:2). Here comes the last occasion of the characteristic phrase "let us," which is found twelve times in this Epistle, all of them possessing special point and force.

(2) *A Call to Good Works* (v. 16).—This is another sacrifice, but of works instead of words. We are to keep in mind continually the duty to well-doing, and of having fellowship with our brother-Christians in all helpful actions, "for with such sacrifices God is well pleased." This divine pleasure is twofold: God is pleased with our faith (11:6), and with our works (13:16).

(3) *A Call to Obedience.*— Already an appeal has been made to recall past teachers (v. 7), and now comes another appeal to obey those who at present have the guidance and control. The description is that of an ideal ministry, "they watch for your souls as they that must give account." Happy the congregation which possesses such a ministry, and happy the ministry which fulfils this requirement. The result will be joy and not grief to the minister, and unspeakable profit to the hearer.

(4) *A Call to Prayer* (vv. 18, 19).— The writer whoever he was, desires to be included in their fellowship of prayer. He feels that he can ask for these remembrances before God because of the consciousness of sincerity in his heart and life, and he is all the more anxious that this should be done in order that he may have the unspeakable joy of a speedier fellowship with them on restoration to liberty. Nothing could be more beautiful than this thought of one praying for another as an essential part of true Christian life.

2. The Special Prayer (vv. 20, 21)

In this closing prayer of doxology, the entire Epistle is summed up, and on this account it calls for the closest possible attention along the following lines:

(1) *Life's Highest Purpose.* "To do His will." Everything is summed up in this simple but searching phrase. This is what God requires.

(2) *Life's Greatest Need.*—"Make you perfect in every good work." The word "perfect" here, unlike the rest of the Epistle, means to adjust or set right. It is said to be a medical term, implying the replacing a joint after dislocation. If the Christian life is to be lived aright, there must be this spiritual adjustment. The same word is found quite frequently in St. Paul's Epistles (I Cor. 1:10; II Cor. 13:11; Gal. 6:1; I Thess. 3:10; II Cor. 13:9; Eph. 4:12; see also Matt. 4:21; I Pet. 5:10). This is what God desires.

(3) *Life's Perfect Profession.*—"Working in you that which is well pleasing in His sight." He has to do His work within our souls (Phil. 2:13), and we may be sure that what He does in this way will be pleasing to Him (11:6; 13:16). This is what God will do.

(4) *Life's Glorious Assurance.*—"The God of peace." This divine title is found several times in the New Testament (Rom. 15:33; 16:20; I Cor. 14:33; II Cor 13:11; I Thess. 5:23), and it is invariably connected with the believer's holiness. The two ideas are associated in 12:14. This is what God is.

(5) *Life's Ample Guarantee.*—"Who brought again from the dead our Lord Jesus, that Great Shepherd of the sheep through the blood of the everlasting covenant." This is the only place in the Epistle where Christ's resurrection is named. The typical character of

the Jewish tabernacle had no place for the resurrection, as distinct from the ascension, and the thought as we have seen passes straight from the death on Calvary to our Lord's appearance in heaven on our behalf. But here where the reference is clearly to the power of God in relation to our life, the resurrection is fitly mentioned. God who brought Christ from the dead is able to bring us. He is here called "the great shepherd." It is one of the three passages where He is spoken of under this figure. He is "the good shepherd" who died (John 10:14), "the great shepherd" who rose (Heb. 13:20), and "the chief shepherd" who will come again (I Pet. 5:4). This is what God has done.

(6) *Life's Simple Secret.* — "Through Jesus Christ." Everything that comes to the believer's life is associated with our Lord. "Through Him" we have access to God (Eph. 2:18), and in this access every needful and conceivable grace becomes ours. This is what God provides.

(7) *Life's Complete Realization.* — "To whom be glory for ever and ever." This is the crowning point of the divine purpose concerning us. "Glory" is the manifestation of splendor, and our lives adjusted to the will of God, and filled with His grace, are to be the expression of His "glory" in time and for eternity. This is what God expects.

3. THE PERSONAL APPEAL (vv. 22-25)

A few purely personal matters fitly close this Letter. He urges that the readers should be ready to allow this "word" of exhortation (v. 22). He tells them of Timothy's freedom, and of the expectation of their meeting with him. He sends greetings from himself and those who are with him (v. 24), and he closes with prayer that divine grace may be with them all.

Looking back over all this section of application, from 10:19, it is possible to see the Christian's privileges (chap. 10), his power (chap. 11), his progress (chap. 12), and his practice (chap. 13).

And so we come to the close of this wonderful Epistle, with its rich, deep, full teaching for the Christian life. The word "Hebrew" is said to mean "one who has crossed over," and the Jews, as represented by their forefather Abraham, and as exemplified in their own national life, may be said to have had a threefold crossing over: the Euphrates, the Red Sea, and the Jordan. The first means that the old life had gone. The second, that the new life was possible. The third, that the new life was to be lived. Spiritually this suggests for the Christian that we are to remember "old things are passed away, behold all things have become new." We are to "draw near," and "draw not back," but "delight ourselves with fatness." Five words may perhaps sum up the entire Epistle from the standpoint of Christian life and duty. We are to enter, to experience, to enjoy, to exult, and to extol.

BIBLIOGRAPHY

COMMENTARIES

The Epistle to the Hebrews — Westcott
Hebrews in The Pulpit Commentary — Barmby and Jerdan
The Holiest of All — Murray
The Epistle to the Hebrews — Chadwick
Hebrews — Davidson
Commentary on Hebrews — Delitzsch (2 vols.)
Hebrews — Peake (Century Bible)
The Epistle to the Hebrews — Edwards (Expositor's Bible)
The Jewish Temple and the Christian Church — Dale
Tait's Exposition of the Hebrews (2 vols.)
The Epistle to the Hebrews — Wickham
The Epistle to the Hebrews — Rendall
Exposition of the Epistle to the Hebrews — Kelly
Olshausen and Ebrard on the Hebrews
Epistle to the Hebrews — Nairne (Cambridge Greek Testament)
The Epistle to the Hebrews — Holmes (Indian Church Commentaries)
Christ Superior to Moses and Aaron — Govett

EXPOSITIONS

Lectures on the Hebrews — Adolph Saphir (2 vols.)
The Way into the Holiest — Meyer
Hebrews — W. Douglas Moffatt
The Twelve-Gemmed Crown — Porter
The Epistle to the Hebrews — Bruce
Studies in Hebrews — Rotherham
The Eternal Inheritance — Radford
High Priesthood and Sacrifice — Du Bose
The Epistle of Priesthood — Nairne
The Hebrews' Epistle — Anderson
Gleanings in the Hebrews — Sprunt
The Supreme Gospel — Kerr
Better Things — Gregory Mantle
Epistle to the Hebrews — Hodgkin
Within the Vail — Simpson
Forster on the Hebrews
The Foundation Stone of Christian Faith — J. Gurney Hoare

STUDIES

We Have An Altar — Edward Doveton (Booklet)
God's Apostle and High Priest — Philip Mauro

185

Leading Ideas on the Epistle to the Hebrews — Bailey
Helps to Studies in the Epistle to the Hebrews — Guy
The Theology of the Epistle to the Hebrews — Milligan
Notes on the Epistle to the Hebrews — Grant
Notes on the Epistle to the Hebrews — J. N. D.
Hebrews: A Catechetical Study — Chapell
Musings on the Epistle to the Hebrews — J. G. B.
Notes on Hebrews — F. E. R.
His Son — Leon Tucker
God's Pilgrims — Philip Mauro
Our High Priest in Heaven — Archdeacon Perowne
The Altar Question in the Light of Holy Scripture—Kemnon (Booklet)
The Golden Altar — Burkett (Booklet)

Date Due

Code 4386-04, CLS-4, Broadman Supplies, Nashville, Tenn.,
Printed in U.S.A.